The *CHEAP$KATE* Next Door

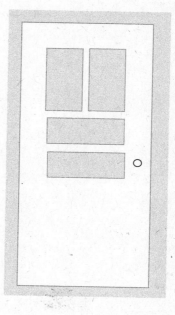

ALSO BY JEFF YEAGER

The Ultimate Cheapskate's Road Map to True Riches

The
CHEAP$KATE
Next Door

THE SURPRISING SECRETS OF AMERICANS
LIVING HAPPILY BELOW THEIR MEANS

Jeff Yeager

Broadway Books
New York

BROADWAY

Copyright © 2010 by Jeffrey Yeager

Published in the United States by Broadway Books, an imprint of the Crown
Publishing Group, a division of Random House, Inc., New York.

www.crownpublishing.com

BROADWAY BOOKS and the Broadway Books colophon are trademarks
of Random House, Inc.

Library of Congress Cataloging-in-Publication Data

Yeager, Jeff.
The cheapskate next door : the surprising secrets of Americans
living happily below their means / Jeff Yeager.—1st ed.
p. cm.
1. Finance, Personal. 2. Thriftiness. I. Title.

HG179.Y426 2010
332.024—dc22   2009042287

ISBN 978-0-7679-3132-8

Printed in the United States of America

10 9 8 7 6 5 4 3 2 1

First Edition

A WORD FROM THE AUTHOR

THE FOLLOWING BOOK is nonfiction. Or, more accurately, what I call "colorized nonfiction."

In an attempt to write a book about the yawn-inducing subject of personal finance that might not only inform but entertain, I have taken the liberty of embellishing certain events, characters, dialogue, and other stuff, all in the hope that it will allow readers to maintain consciousness—and maybe even have a laugh or two—throughout the reading process. That said, the characters and stories discussed in the pages ahead are ultimately based on real people and real events, particularly those that will seem most surreal to non-cheapskate readers.

Also be advised that—because cheapskates down through the ages have been unjustly singled out for public ridicule—some of the individuals mentioned in this book are enrolled in the CIPP (Cheapskate Identity Protection Program), and their names have been changed at their request. Any similarity between those individuals and other people sharing the same names, whether living or dead, cheapskate or spendthrift, is purely coincidental.

Like most books about personal finance, this one is intended as a general guide. You should seek the advice of a qualified personal finance professional about your individual financial situation and plans. Come to think of it, you may just have a "qualified personal finance professional" living right next door—if he or she is a cheapskate.

—Jeff Yeager,
The Ultimate Cheapskate

To my parents, Joyce and Doug Yeager, and to all parents who teach their children that happiness is not about money. That priceless-but-free gift you give your kids becomes more valuable with each passing year. This I know, thanks to my mom and dad.

CONTENTS

The Dawning of the Age
of the Cheapskate

My first book, *The Ultimate Cheapskate's Road Map to True Riches*, came out in 2008. Ironically, that was also the year that the U.S. economy imploded. The Age of the Cheapskate started just about the very day that my little book hit the shelves.

But I'll always remember 2008 as the year I slept in some mighty strange places. I hit the road in early January, shortly after *Road Map* was released, on a series of book-tours-by-bicycle, cleverly dubbed the "Tour de Cheapskate." I bicycled nearly 3,000 miles on those trips (bringing my lifetime pedaling total to more than 85,000 miles), and I traveled many thousands more by plane, bus, train, and occasionally functioning rental car over the course of the year.

I convinced my publisher to let me travel on the cheap, not just bicycling but staying in the homes of fellow cheapskates and other total strangers I found through CouchSurfing.com. I wanted to take what I saved the publisher on my expenses and donate it to local libraries along my tour routes. At first the publisher was skeptical. They asked me, "Jeff, do you think it will be safe?" I assured them that I had no intention of hurting anyone or stealing anything from the folks who were kind enough to put me up along the way.

The venture raised nearly $3,000 for public libraries and other local nonprofit groups, but I admit that along those many miles I had my moments of doubt. When I couldn't find a cheapskate's couch to crash on for the night, I'd often pitch my tent along some lonesome highway, falling asleep to the sound of passing semi trucks and the late-night howls of beer-swilling teenagers in their souped-up Chevys.

One night in Ohio I was camped in a dry creek bed just off a bridge abutment, when a group of late-night party animals just happened to select that very spot, on that very bridge, on that very night, to stop their car and relieve their beer-laden bladders into the darkness over the side of the bridge. Their tinkle fell on my tent fly like raindrops on a lily pad, the urinators never the wiser for it. The next night I made sure to set up camp *under* the bridge.

Once in southern Florida, it looked to be a perfect night to sleep under the stars, so I rolled my sleeping bag out on the velvety green grass in a small public park. I slept soundly all night, face down on the manicured lawn. But as dawn broke, I felt the most horrifying physical sensation of my life. It felt as if all the internal organs in my abdomen had spontaneously ruptured—like someone was taking a Mixmaster to them—and I was suddenly hemorrhaging by the bucketful.

I jumped to my feet, half trying to shake off the nightmare, half expecting to see myself covered in blood, but the blood was clear, like water. Only then did I realize that the park's automatic sprinklers were set to come on at dawn, and a pop-up sprinkler head had been strategically located directly under my navel as I'd slept peacefully. The next night I treated myself to a Motel 6.

And while I will always love and appreciate each and every one of the kind folks who opened their homes to me along the way, many of those home stays came with stories of their own. Like the time I stayed with an elderly couple during my tour of the Southwest desert. Waking up in the middle of the night in unfamiliar surroundings, I felt the midnight thirst that often comes with long-distance cycling. I needed water, *now.*

Stumbling into the bathroom, unable to find the light switch, I finally fumbled upon a drinking glass on the nightstand next to the sink. I filled the glass in the dark with the coldest water the tap could deliver, and then tipped it back and chugged the whole thing without stopping—well, until I reached the bottom of the glass, that is, and a pair of dentures belonging to one of my hosts came sliding along with the last gulp. The next morning I skipped breakfast.

Most of all, I slept in lots and lots of kids' bedrooms, and I want to once again thank all of the kids across the country who were evicted from their rooms by their parents when the Ultimate Cheapskate came to spend the night. I spent so many nights in these now-familiar surroundings that I can exactly describe the requisite decor of a child's bedroom circa 2008:

- A galaxy of glow-all-night-long stars and planets (including multiple Saturns) pasted on the ceiling above the bed
- A snake or other amphibian/reptilian thing lurking in a not-so-secure-looking aquarium in the corner
- Regardless of the child's gender, an Asian boy band's poster staring at me each morning when I awoke in the munchkin-sized bed, my half-naked 6′4″ frame hanging out from under a Shrek bedspread

Several weeks into my tour, I woke one morning in a kid's bedroom and caught a glimpse of myself in the mirror, a paunchy profile shot, wearing only boxer shorts. I did a double take. I could have sworn I had morphed into Shrek overnight. The next day I bought myself some real pajamas and went on a diet.

The primary purpose of the Tour de Cheapskate was to promote my *Road Map to True Riches*. But I hadn't pedaled very far before I realized that another book was emerging out of the experiences I was having, the people I was meeting, and the financial upheavals that were rocking the U.S. and world economies on a daily basis.

At first I tried to put the thought of writing another book out of my mind, since I was still plenty spent from writing the first one. Sixty-five thousand words is a lot for a guy like me with a very limited vocabulary. That's why I used so many of the same words more than once in *Road Map*. But the idea just kept chafing inside me, like the saddle on my ten-speed was chafing my backside.

As I sat around countless kitchen tables, breaking bread, swapping stories, and exchanging frugal philosophies with the cheapskates who invited me into their homes, I was learning more than I ever imagined I would. Going into the tour, I thought I knew everything there is to know about thrift and what I call the "cheapskate lifestyle." I expected that most folks who hosted me would be, well, a lot like me. I believed that all cheapskates were cut out of the same sackcloth.

That theory had the air let out of it even before I had my first flat tire, less than a week into the first leg of the Tour de Cheapskate. What I was finding was a tremendous diversity of lifestyles, backgrounds, attitudes, and beliefs among the frugal folks who invited me into their lives.

No two families or individuals I visited seemed to be the same, yet they were all proud, self-proclaimed "cheapskates," at least under the terms and definitions I'd laid out in *Road Map*. My readers, I was finding, were not at all who or what I thought they'd be.

But then I began to scratch beneath the surface, and not because of that bed of fire ants I'd set up my tent on back in Yuma. I began to scratch beneath the outward veneers and lifestyle differences of the people I was meeting. That's when I began discovering *the secrets.*

What I began to realize was that despite their wide range of lifestyles, family situations, and personal beliefs, the people I'd met—and hundreds more I would meet and correspond with in the months to come—had in common a set of vitally important practices and philosophies when it came to money and the role money plays in their lives. They know how to live happily, but in a most nontraditional American style: The cheapskate next door knows the secrets of how to *live happily below one's means.*

As I got to know them and slept in their homes during some of the toughest economic times since the Great Depression, what struck me most was that the cheapskates I met were sleeping soundly at night at a time when so many Americans were losing sleep in an economy gone haywire. The secrets of my cheapskate brothers and sisters, their knowledge of how to live happily below their means, had largely insulated them from the raging economic inferno sweeping the country.

That's when I knew that I *must* write this book, to share those secrets at a time in our nation's history when they're needed most, at a time when they can help so many Americans.

In writing this book I also reflected on my own frugality and upbringing. I realized that because of them, I, too, was sleeping soundly at night during tough times. Even on those nights when someone was peeing on my tent.

ACKNOWLEDGMENTS

I like to write the acknowledgments last, after the manuscript is complete. That way I can take advantage of every remaining page the publisher will allow me to thank everyone involved. My greatest fear is that I'll inadvertently leave someone out, so I apologize in advance if I do.

The profound anxiety I felt as I sat down to write this book was in knowing that I could never fully capture and celebrate the collective wisdom of my worldwide network of volunteer Miser Advisers, my beloved bargain-basement brain trust. These are the folks who actually wrote this book—I just copied it down—every time they returned one of my ten-page questionnaires, invited me into their homes, sat with me for an interview, or spoke with me over the phone (thanks again for accepting my collect calls).

So, to my cherished Miser Advisers, thank you one and all. You're the best. But just remember, I'll always be the cheapest.

A great many Miser Advisers and other folks went above and beyond the call of their cheapskate duty in providing input and encouragement on this project, including: Dorraine Darden, Jerry Dyson, Kate Easlick, Kelly Kamann, Carol McAnulty, Steve McCullough, Becka and Justin Miller, Bob Moyers, Daniel Newman and Bruce Ostyn, Mike and Tara Overpeck and family, Jacquie Phelan, Lona and Gordon Powell and family, Donna and Tim Rodgers and family, Nancy Saint John, Ray Sola, Gerald and Julia Thomson, Steve Weigel, Amy Williams, and my brother, Joel Yeager, who allowed me ample latitude in recounting stories from our childhood.

Like all good cheapskates, I hate debt. But I owe a huge debt of gratitude to all those I work with in the book publishing business. Among many others, thank you: Kristine Puopolo, my extraordinary editor-in-cheap, who shockingly allowed me to use a record seventeen exclamation marks in the 230+ pages ahead; David Drake, the guru of publicity at Broadway Books, who let me undertake the 2008 Tour de Cheapskate when conventional business wisdom said *nada*; and Stacey Glick, my unflappable literary agent, who has the unenviable task of representing America's cheapest author.

I'd also like to thank all those in the media who give me a chance to spread the gospel of cheap on a regular basis, including the good folks at: NBC's *Today* show, TheDailyGreen.com (where I blog weekly), *Bottom Line Personal, Writer's Digest*, WiseBread.com, Authentic Entertainment, and *AARP The Magazine*, television, and online). And a special thanks to my fellow writers at the *Writer's Digest* online community (forum.writersdigest.com), where every day we help each other become better writers and keep each other's hopes and dreams alive. Write on.

Being the new kid on the block when it comes to personal finance writers, I guess I wasn't surprised to find that this business is just like most others: Some people go out of their way to help you, while others won't even return your calls. Thank you, Jean Chatzky, Gary Foreman, Gregory Karp, Stephanie Nelson, Vicki Robin, J. D. Roth, Michelle Singletary, and many others in this business who did me so many good turns when I was first starting out.

Finally, none of the joy in my life would be possible without the loving companionship and constant good humor of Denise, my pooooor wife of twenty-six years, who helped me such a great deal with this book. Can you imagine being married to America's Cheapest Man? Denise is a true saint to put up with me. That's why I dedicated my first book to her. Of course, I'm still hoping that someday she'll fork over the $12.95 and have a chance to read it.

No joke, De De. You know you rock my reduced-for-quick-sale world, and I'm gonna love you forever.

The *CHEAP$KATE* Next Door

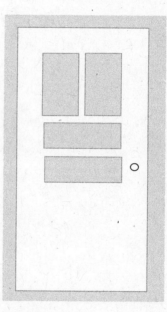

Cheapskates:
They're Everywhere and They're Loving Life

Once we're above the survival level, the difference between prosperity and poverty lies simply in our degree of gratitude.

—*Your Money or Your Life*, by Joe Dominguez and Vicki Robin

Sure, we could afford to spend more, but why would we? It wouldn't make us any happier."

That's it.

That's the simple statement that I've spent the last year and a half traveling the country to hear.

Those words have been my touchstone. That's what this book is about, and it's what the cheapskates next door have to share with you. They can show you how to live *happily* below your means.

"Don't touch the testicles! Besides, they're too hot to eat right now anyhow."

My longtime friend and fellow cheapskate Clive Jenkins is an extreme case, both as a friend, cheapskate, and roast-master of whole lambs, pigs, and various other mammals he occasionally prepares in his backyard on a grilling rig he fashioned out of an old oil drum, cement blocks from a garage he tore down, and spare parts from his kids' bicycles.

Please don't judge all cheapskates by my friend Clive. He's a great guy, but most of us cheapskates are probably a whole lot more like you than we are like Clive. At least I hope so.

The idea of spending less than you earn—*living below your means*—seems like simple common sense. Figure out what your take-home pay is, and then make it a point to spend less than that every month. Take what you don't spend, and save it for emergencies, big-ticket items you can't afford to pay for out of your regular paychecks, or long-term goals like retirement or sending a child to college. What could be simpler, right?

Guess again. We live in a country where the norm is to do just the opposite, to spend *more* than you earn. By the end of 2007, household debt in the United States reached a record 133.7 percent of disposable income. Disposable income is gross income after taxes, so if the average family spent every after-tax penny they earned just on eliminating their personal debt, it would take about one and one-third years for them to be debt-free. The average U.S. household with at least one credit card has nearly $10,700 in credit card debt. College students who graduated with student loans in 2007 owed an average of almost $23,000 on those loans, plus they already had credit card debt of their own of more than $2,200. Nothing like starting young, I suppose.

Our addiction to borrowing, the mechanism through which we're able to spend more than we earn, and our aversion to saving some of what we earn for the proverbial rainy day, are both fairly recent trends in America. Total consumer debt grew nearly eight times in size from 1980 ($355 billion) to 2008 ($2.6 trillion). During that same period, the share of disposable income each household spent servicing its consumer debt and mortgage debt increased by 35 percent.

Once upon a time in America, the way we accumulated savings was by, well, spending less than we made and banking the difference. In 1982, the average household put 11 percent of its disposable income into savings; twenty-five years later that figure had dropped to less than 1 percent. In those years, we came to accept as gospel (at least up until recently) that the way smart people build wealth is through the appreciation of their assets, particularly their homes. Spending less, staying out of debt, and socking away some of your paycheck—those antiquated wealth-building techniques fell out of fashion faster than runners-up on *American Idol.*

Not too long ago, we used to live—and spend money—very differently. For example, in 1981 between two-thirds and three-quarters of all housewares we purchased were to replace a worn-out item. Now those figures are roughly reversed, with the vast majority of such purchases being "wants" rather than "needs." The old *whatever-it-is* we already own still works fine, but we want a new one, maybe the latest style, maybe a different color. I call this fairly recent transformation of our shopping habits "*wantonizing* our needs."

Today, spending less than they earn seems to be very difficult for a lot of people. Maybe you think it's impossible for you, too. But go back and reread the first two sentences of this chapter; living like the cheapskate next door is not only a question of living below your means, of spending less than you earn, and of avoiding debt whenever possible. It's just as much about being *happy*— truly happy, joyous really—with a lifestyle of less that feels like more.

It's the "happy" part of the equation that I hope sets this book apart from so many others that have been written about spending less money. The lessons of this book—the secrets of the cheapskate next door—are as much about happiness as they are about money. For cheapskates like me, you will learn, money really has very little to do with true happiness. By spending and consuming wisely, we make money a relatively minor part of our lives. We worry less about money than most people, and we can afford the luxury of spending fewer of our limited hours here on Earth chasing after ever more of it. We can focus our time and our attention on the truly valuable things in life—those that often come without a price tag—like spending time with the ones we love, helping others, and pursuing our passions. Because we consume things sparingly, thoughtfully, and fully, things do not consume us.

So I hope you'll approach this book not so much as a survival guide for tough times, but rather as a *revival guide*—a way of reviving your non-monetary soul and finding happiness by spending and consuming less.

We've Come a Long Way, Baby

In good economic times, when high-paying jobs are plentiful and our investments are kicking butt, living *within* your means—let alone *below* your means—is a pretty unpopular notion for most people. Credit is easy to come by, so we can borrow money to get whatever we want, the minute we want it. And since home values always go up, the stock market is recession proof, and I can always go out and find another job that will pay me even more than the one I have now, what's the problem?

In 2008, we learned some lessons the hard way. United States households' net worth nosedived by about 18 percent or $11 trillion, an amount equal to the annual gross national product of Japan, Germany, and the United Kingdom combined. The foreclosure frenzy began as home values declined nearly 30 percent

from their peak levels in 2006, resulting in fourteen million homeowners owing more on their mortgages than their homes were
worth. More than 1.2 million people filed for bankruptcy in 2008,
and in 2009 unemployment rates climbed to a twenty-five-year
high.

"Shock and awe" barely describes what's happened to the economy. Downward trends turned into a downward spiral and then
into a literal free fall that would make the oxygen masks drop out
of the overhead compartments on a Boeing 747. It's a whole new
economy.

Who would have thought a few years ago that Ken Lay's Enron
would begin to look like a model for good corporate management?
That during the Christmas shopping season of 2008, I would swear
I saw then–U.S. Treasury Secretary Henry Paulson in my local
dollar store? I was shocked to discover that Cabinet members are
apparently allowed to moonlight.

Everything has changed in this new economy, even our language. Marketers invented the term "under-buyers" to refer to
those people who are now spending less—either less than they did
before or less than they can afford. I guess they thought the word
"cheapskate" would hurt people's feelings.

Yes, when it comes to the economy, we've come a long way,
baby. And it's all been downhill. Or has it? It's a new economy now,
and I believe it is inviting us to take a new approach to money, and
to life.

Please, Just Call Me *Cheap* . . . "Under-Buyer" Sounds So Negative

What do you think of when you think of a "cheapskate"? Probably
someone who's greedy, like Ebenezer Scrooge; someone who's con-

stantly worrying about saving a penny, and who leads a joyless life because of it. Maybe even someone who's dishonest, who thrives on gaming the system and taking advantage of others.

In my first book, *The Ultimate Cheapskate's Road Map to True Riches*, I tried to dispel those negative connotations. The basic premise of that book is my heartfelt belief that most Americans would be happier, and the quality of their lives would actually increase, if they would only spend and consume less. *Road Map* is about the potentially life-changing realization that less can often be more, and that by being a cheapskate you can choose to value your time, and the things you can do with it, more than money and the things you can buy with it.

To me, a cheapskate is the polar opposite of a conspicuous consumer. You remember conspicuous consumers, don't you? Those are the folks who are finally falling out of fashion these days. The ones who were last seen heading off in their Hummer, hoping to grab their eighty-four-inch plasma screen TV off the living room wall before the bank foreclosed on their seven-thousand-square-foot home in Ain't We Sumpthin' Hills.

Conspicuous consumers spend and consume stuff at warp speed (primarily to show others that they can do so). Cheapskates, on the other hand, are too self-confident—and frankly too smart—to spend money on things they don't need and probably don't even want, simply to impress others or just because they can.

Who Is the Cheapskate Next Door?

The day *Road Map* hit the shelves, the cheapskates started coming out of the back aisles of the dollar store. They put down the how-to books they were reading at the public library. They rose up from the fifty-cent piles at their favorite local thrift stores.

Cheapskates from across the country began writing, e-mailing, and even phoning me—on their own dime!—to unite under the banner of the Cheap Pride movement I kicked off in the final chapter of *Road Map*. My wife kidded me that it was like being King of the Gypsies, the leader of a nation of people who are proud and united citizens, but who lack an actual country they can call home.

Jacquie Phelan, who was a Freegan (aka "dumpster diver") long before there was such a thing as a Freegan, wrote from the San Francisco Bay Area to introduce herself, cleverly using a postcard that was actually two postcards taped back to back. She'd doubled the return on her single twenty-seven-cent stamp investment, and did me the courtesy of providing an easy, inexpensive way to reply. My Inner Miser immediately fell in love with Jacquie, and that was even before I saw the calendar photos of her riding her mountain bike wearing nothing but mud.

Families of every size and background from across the country, like Donna and Tim Rodgers and their five kids, contacted me to say that they enjoyed *Road Map* very much, and they wanted me to know that it's indeed possible to raise a large family on a small income, and to be blissfully happy while doing it. They invited me to visit them in Texas so that they could show me how it's done. They were hoping that my next book would put the lie to the notion that raising a large family requires spending on a level rivaling the national debt.

Couples in their thirties and forties, like Gerald and Julia Thomson of Phoenix, Arizona, wrote to me about their imminent plans to retire early, not because they'd earned so much money during their careers, but because they knew how to live happily below their means.

Young newlyweds contacted me to share their techniques for

living the good life on less, like Becka and Justin Miller, who manage to live comfortably in their dream home on a very modest income. That home, by the way, is a forty-eight-foot steel-hulled sailing ship anchored in beautiful Baltimore Harbor that they're buying for a mere $18,000. Talk about knowing a secret or two.

College students called me (sometimes in the wee hours of the morning, reeking of beer . . . yes, even over the phone) to say they'd just finished reading my book and that it was the first personal finance book they'd ever read. "I think it's gonna change my life, man. And, oh yeah, is that Coach Sacstretcher dude a real guy?" (Coach Sacstretcher was a prominent figure in my first book and makes a cameo appearance or two in this one.)

Bruce Ostyn and his partner, Daniel Newman, e-mailed me to say that I'd ruined their evening of reading aloud to each other. The longtime couple makes a sport of picking apart personal finance books (particularly those in the make-some-more-money-so-you-can-buy-some-more-stuff genre), but they'd found little to criticize in *Road Map*. The self-employed interior designers invited me to visit them at their home in Arizona to show me how "cheap" and "style" are anything but mutually exclusive. They could tell from the photo on the book jacket that I needed some serious fashion help.

And Pastor Mike Overpeck at the Waterford Community Church in Goshen, Indiana, delivered a sermon on my book. At first that news concerned me, given my occasional use of rough language and off-color humor in *Road Map*. I assumed the sermon was to encourage the burning of my book. (On second thought, if they wanted to buy up the entire first edition at $12.95 a copy and light a match to it, who am I to complain?) It turned out that Overpeck had challenged his entire congregation to go on one of my "fiscal fasts"—going for a week without spending any money—and he wanted to share with me the positive, community-building impact that the exercise had had on his congregation.

Who are the cheapskates next door? They are single, and they're married. They're young, middle-aged, and they're old. They have small families, and they have huge families. They live in the sticks, suburbs, and cities. They're black, white, yellow, and brown. They run the range from devoted Christians to avowed atheists, from Reagan Republicans to Obama Democrats, and every stripe in between.

Some have six-figure incomes and a seven-figure net worth. Others earn so little that they could qualify for public assistance, but they choose not to since they feel they have more than enough on which to live a good life.

They're a cross-section of America, but what they have in common is that they all live happily below their means. They are the cheapskates next door, and the greatest reward I received as a result of writing *Road Map*—and truly one of the greatest experiences of my life—has been getting the chance to meet and know them.

But like any book, *Road Map* also has its critics. Some readers complained, for instance, that the fact that my wife and I don't have children makes some of the advice in *Road Map* less valuable, or even impractical, for families with kids. And some critics, including one with the *New York Times*, seemed to feel that my occasional idiosyncrasies—like my fondness for dining on meats of the offal variety—classify me as more of a nut job than a personal finance writer. Fair enough, everyone's entitled to their opinions, but I still like liver.

So, in sitting down to write this book, I was determined to show the breadth of lifestyle choices and family situations that are possible if you know the secrets for happily living below your means. It's not about adopting the Yeagers' lifestyle, or choosing not to have children, or forcing yourself to eat tripe (although it is delicious, by the way. Just ask Clive).

This book is about realizing that there's a person or a family out there—*just like you*—who is spending a lot less money and consuming a lot less stuff than you probably do in your own life. And here's the real kicker: They're probably happier (maybe even much, much happier) than you are because of it. That's because they know some secrets that you don't.

Looking for a Few Good Cheapskates

In order to collect all the stories and ideas that my cheapskate brothers and sisters were so anxious to share, I decided to develop a simple questionnaire for willing cheapskates to complete. Given my background in nonprofit management—where no task is so simple that, with sufficient effort, it can't be made complicated—this document quickly morphed into a ten-page, four-thousand-word behemoth, the Moby-Dick of questionnaires. If you're up for a cheap challenge, I've posted an annotated version of the official Cheapskate Next Door Questionnaire on my website, Ultimate Cheapskate.com, so you can see how you stack up against the cheapskate next door.

At first I fretted that no one would take the three to five hours typically needed to complete the questionnaire, but I was convinced that I needed more than just a peek inside the lives of the cheapskates next door. If I was going to distill the essential secrets for living happily below one's means, I needed to see and understand the whole enchilada when it came to their finances, lifestyles, beliefs, and practices.

The first lesson I learned was to never underestimate the determination and resolve of the cheapskate next door when it comes to wanting to tell you about how *they* do things. In fact, early on in the process I was able to clinically diagnose the psychological condition now known as Tightwad Envy, or *Skinflintus Invidia* in Latin. TE is a psychological condition whereby a cheapskate's natural sense of pride regarding their own thriftiness and frugal practices manifests itself in an unhealthy level of competitiveness toward the thrift-craft of others.

And so I was inundated, like a grocery store flooded with cheapskates on triple-coupon day, by hundreds of fully completed questionnaires and hundreds of other comments and messages from cheapskates, all chomping at the bit to share their secrets and the details of their lives. Dozens upon dozens also invited me to visit them in their homes, and, as I've said previously, it was one of the greatest experiences of my life to take many of them up on that generous offer.

Who the Cheapskate Next Door *Isn't*

From those thousands of pages of questionnaires, interview notes, and other correspondence from cheapskates around the country, their secrets for happily living below one's means began to emerge. I discovered many new ideas, and found out things about their lives and families that surprised me time and again.

But what I didn't find was the kind of miserable, greedy, unscrupulous, Grinch-like cheapskate you might imagine. That's not to say that such individuals don't exist, but they're not the type of proud, generous, self-actualized individuals I found to be the norm, and on whom this book is based.

In all of my research and travels, I came across only a handful of people who clearly led an unhappy, wretched life because of their zeal to save money. For the vast majority, the decision to live below their means was, perhaps surprisingly, really not about money at all. Their attitudes and approaches to money were most often grounded in something bigger, such as spiritual, religious, or ethical beliefs. They weren't hoarders or people intent on amassing a large bank account for the sake of having a large bank account. Rather, they were people who were content, by and large, with what they already had.

Thankfully, I encountered even fewer people who were dishonest in their attempts to save money, because that type of behavior has no place in this book. Those are the kind of people who give cheapskates a bad name.

For example, one fellow who travels a lot on business proudly told me that he always brings with him his burned-out lightbulbs from home so that he can swap them out for working lightbulbs in the hotel rooms where he stays. He also bragged about stealing pool towels (which usually aren't inventoried) and entire rolls of toilet paper from hotels.

Even when he's at home, he routinely makes the rounds of local hotels that offer a "free continental breakfast," generously helping himself under the premise that the sign out front doesn't specify "for hotel guests only." By the end of our conversation, I wasn't sure he was a cheapskate so much as a kleptomaniac with a hotel fetish. Regardless, things like that are just wrong, and he'll probably spend eternity at the Bates Motel because of it.

Still, I can't deny that some of the cheapskates I've met have been plenty colorful, though in a friendly and good-spirited sort of way. I'll also admit that some of the tips they've shared with me come with a pretty high *yuck* factor, even for an offal fan like me.

Like the older woman I spoke to who saves her used Q-tips and uses them to detail her car—inside and out ("They have just the right amount of [ear] wax on them"). Or a cheapskate neighbor of mine who cleans out his own septic tank ("All 520 bucketsful!" he boasts proudly, as if it's a *Guinness* world record for poop-scooping). And, even without being asked, more than one of my cheapskate brothers and sisters indicated that wearing underwear was an optional extravagance, "at least between May and September," as one woman told me (I interviewed her in July).

Okay, so maybe some of the cheapskates next door are a bit über-frugal, but that's part of their charm.

Different Paths to the Same Destination

If you want to see cheapskates argue, put a bunch of us in a room together and ask us about shopping at dollar stores or membership warehouse clubs. You'll probably get as many different opinions as there are tightwads in the room.

And don't even get us started about coupons. As many cheapskates seem to swear by coupons as swear about them. For some, coupon clipping is almost a holy ritual, a sort of *budgetary bris*, and they proudly produce their sacred scrolls of cash-register receipts to document their savings. Other cheapskates are convinced that most coupons only encourage you to buy unnecessary items, take too much time to clip and redeem, and most often are a false value.

But such difference in the tactics of thrift have convinced me that there is no one right way to shop for bargains, manage your paycheck, or ultimately achieve happiness while living below your means. There are many tactics and approaches that are valuable, and thus are included in this book. Because of that variety, you'll likely find a method that will work for you, in your own particular situation and lifestyle.

While their tactics vary more than the fans in line at a Santana concert, what struck me most about the cheapskates I surveyed were the commonalities among them. Some of these things will probably come as no surprise: They despise debt and they've found ways to either pay it off or keep it out of their lives in the first place. They often buy used, and rarely pay full retail price. They tend to stay around home more, at least when it comes to avoiding expensive outings like dining out or going to professional sporting events.

Others will likely catch you off guard. For example, most cheapskates claim that they think, argue, and stress out *less* about money than most other people they know, contradicting the popular image of pensive penny-pinchers who lead a life focused on money. And believe it or not, price is usually not the most important consideration when they shop, refuting the old definition of a cheapskate as "someone who knows the price of everything, but the value of nothing."

On most of the major financial issues in life, such as buying a home, financing big-ticket items like cars and a college education, and raising children, I found a high degree of consensus among cheapskates. However, the cheapskate approach to these Big Kahuna issues is usually dramatically different from the course taken by most Americans, and often contrary to the advice given by many personal financial pundits. For example:

- Roughly 85 percent of cheapskates polled said they plan to pay off their home mortgages early or already have.
- More than five out of every six cheapskates buy their automobiles used instead of new, often paying cash instead of taking out a loan.
- They teach their children about money and frugality from a young age, and if you're a cheapskate's kid you're going to *earn* your weekly allowance (assuming you get one at all).

- They believe strongly in the value of a college education for their children, but feel equally strong about how to pay for that education: The kids need to shoulder much of the burden, and don't even think about taking out a student loan.
- They spend considerably less than the typical American family on food, clothing, and recreation, and way, way, way less on dining out.
- They equate "debt" with "cancer," "imprisonment," and "death."

Sounds like a miserable life, doesn't it? But oddly enough, the divorce rate among married cheapskates is about half the national average. Go figure.

What's more, whether for economic, environmental and/or other reasons, cheapskates waste far fewer resources by wearing things out, using things up, and sometimes simply doing without. For example:

- They report throwing away only about 10 percent of the amount of food most Americans toss out.
- They rarely replace an item unless it's worn out and can't be repaired, which is why . . .
- Most of them still proudly wear a couple of pieces of clothing that they bought during the Carter administration.
- They side with the underdog—literally—being nearly one hundred times more likely to own a pet they found as a stray, or adopted from an animal shelter, than they are to buy one at a pet store or from a breeder.
- They're far more likely to own a Crock-Pot than a plasma screen television, to have a clothesline than an iPod, and a good many of them join hands with me in being among the few non-cave-dwelling holdouts yet to own a cell phone.

And, as my publisher knows all too well from the mysteriously flaccid sales of my first book, lots of cheapskates are avid readers . . . but they usually borrow their books from the public library rather than buy a copy of their own. Oh well, *c'est la cheapskate.*

Let's Go Talk to the Cheapskate Next Door, Shall We?

I read a lot of books. Or, rather, like many people, I *start* to read a lot of books.

I sometimes think that my attention span was permanently shortened by the self-inflicted trauma I suffered as a child, unable to ever fully fall asleep at night for fear that my brother would abscond with my Michigan bankroll, which was tucked away in my George Jetson lunchbox under the bed. (Oh, if only I had that lunchbox today, I'd be getting rich on eBay.)

So when I sit down to write a book, I'm rarely able to write an entire chapter at a time. I find myself writing a little bit here, then a few paragraphs in another chapter, and so on. Someone asked me in an interview the other day, "What's the hardest thing about writing a book?" For once, I didn't have to think very long. "It's the words," I said. "Coming up with all those words, and then having to put them in the right order." Oddly enough, page numbers always come quite easily to me. But I digress.

The result of my writing style is a book that is rather like a Chinese menu. Unlike many personal finance books that painstakingly take you through each of the 447 official, sequential steps to financial salvation, mine can be read in bits and pieces, a little at a time. By all means, adopt those suggestions you like, and ignore those you don't; you'll still come out ahead. Dollar-stretching tips and advice from the cheapskates next door are laced throughout the pages ahead, with some special money-saving strategies highlighted as "Cheap Shots" in each chapter. If you're already a member of the Cheaphood, I'm sure you've heard some of these tightwad tidbits before. But heck, even if only a single idea is new to you, it'll more than pay for this book.

So hang on to your wallet and put away your purse. You won't need them during our visit with The Cheapskate Next Door.

CHAPTER 1

The Phrenology of Frugality:
16 Idiosyncrasies of the Cheapskate Mind

The statistics on sanity are that one out of every four Americans is suffering from some form of mental illness. Think of your three best friends. If they are okay, then it's you.
—Rita Mae Brown

A re you saying that people will be happier if they shop *less?*" Judging from the way she was sneering at me across the faux-news desk, it was clear that the local noonday TV anchorwoman wasn't asking a rhetorical question. She looked like she'd bought—and was wearing—one of everything that QVC was selling that day. And her clothes clearly weren't all she'd bought. Her extensive cosmetic surgery reminded me of a roadside billboard I once saw for a plastic surgeon just across the border in Mexico: "U Pay 4 UR Face + Hips . . . I do UR Breasts 4 Free!"

I'd endeared myself to her earlier by arriving for the interview on my bicycle, in a sweat-stained T-shirt. Suffice it to say that we came from different worlds.

"But shopping is what we *do*. Shopping is what makes us happy. *Are you crazy?*" she said, looking at me like I must have been hitting the box wine in the green room before the interview.

Well, the cheapskate's brain is definitely wired differently, of that I'm convinced. You don't need to spend much time around us or be trained as a psychiatrist (or local news anchor) to figure that out. Whether we're born that way or we pick up certain attitudes and beliefs about life as we go along, the cheapskate next door sees the world a bit differently than most folks.

Here's a brief tour of the cheapskate mindset—a synopsis of the sixteen key synapses that set the cheapskate next door apart from the typical American consumer.

1. The Joneses Can Kiss Our Assets

"Welcome to the Taj Mahovel!" Jacquie Phelan greeted me with a big smile and friendly hug on the doorstep of the eclectic house in Fairfax, California, where she's lived with her husband, Charlie, for the past twenty-six years.

As I'd driven down their street, I had trouble spotting addresses on the immaculately maintained, über-yuppiefied, overly remodeled houses that lined the pleasant lane. But when I saw the warren of little outbuildings strung together by pergolas constructed of every type of salvaged material imaginable, I knew I'd arrived at Jacquie's house. This was clearly the house of someone who wasn't concerned about what the Joneses think. This house had to belong to a cheapskate.

"A few years ago we heard a realtor walking past our house with some prospective buyers, and they were talking about how tacky some of the homes on the street are," Jacquie told me as we sat having lunch under a lean-to made of scrap lumber (aka "The Habitat") in their jungly side yard. "And I piped back to the real estate agent from inside the Habitat, 'It's going to stay that way, too!'"

My lunch with Jacquie and Charlie, by the way, was chicken soup and a truly tasty array of little finger foods, most of which my Freegan hostess told me she'd salvaged the previous evening from dumpsters behind area markets. "Hmm . . . trash-can tapas," I thought to myself. "There's a first time for everything." (Among other journalistic enterprises, Jacquie writes about her unique approach to food and cooking on her blog, "Salivation Army," at phelanfood.wordpress.com.)

Don't get me wrong: Jacquie and Charlie's house isn't a public hazard or anything like that. In fact, it's kind of cool and rather pretty in its own Hobbit-treehouse-ish way. It's just that it's a house designed to please the people who live in it, and not necessarily the people who live next door to it. According to Jacquie, it's also the couple's personal attempt to help "stem the seemingly inevitable shift of the neighborhood from a cozy place, filled with humble homes" into one of "investment (properties) for upwardly mobile but of course deeply-in-debt people" who have no time to become part of the community—and no intention of staying there once they can afford to move on and gentrify the next modest-but-content neighborhood.

Will Rogers once said, "Too many people spend money they haven't earned, to buy things they don't want, to impress people they don't like." Well, he wasn't talking about the cheapskates next door.

When asked the question "On a scale of one to ten, with one being *not important at all* and ten *extremely important*, how concerned are you about 'keeping up with the Joneses' (i.e., maintaining economic status/appearances with your peers)?" roughly 85 percent of cheapskates ranked it as "one," not important at all. (Incidentally, of the remaining 15 percent of respondents, more than half took the liberty of going off the chart and rating it as a "zero" or even less!)

Because of the cheapskates' strong sense of self-worth, they rarely covet the lifestyle or material possessions of others, and have little desire to try to impress other people or keep up appearances. Dylan Davis, of Twinsburg, Ohio, wrote: "We make more money than almost everyone we know, but spend less than all of our peers . . . neither of us cares what other people think about us."

That's not to say that cheapskates are always immune to peer pressure. And luckily, there are things you can do to ward off the big green monster when he does come calling.

Gerald Thomson told me about a time when his wife, Julia, came home from work feeling a little envious of the big homes some of her coworkers were buying. "She sat down at the computer and submitted our financial information to see how much of a mortgage we could qualify for. Once she saw that we *could* qualify to purchase a larger home, she felt better. As long as she knew we could keep up with the Joneses, but choose not to, she was able to keep focused on our early retirement goals."

2. A Cheapskate Values Time More than Money

In my conversations with the cheapskates next door, I was struck by how often they spoke about the value and cost of things not in terms of dollars and cents, but rather days and hours. It's like cheapskates have their own currency. They automatically convert the price of things into the currency of time—their own time.

We've always heard that "time is money." Cheapskates tend to reverse that axiom, making it "money is time." A new pair of boots might cost $150, but for Clara, the cheapskate who makes $32,000 a year, those boots cost close to two days of her time spent working in a job that she doesn't really enjoy. When Clara looks at it in those terms and considers what else she might do with that time and that money, she decides that her old boots will do just fine.

The idea of translating money into the cost of your time was popularized—and maybe pioneered—by Vicki Robin and the late Joe Dominguez in their bestselling book *Your Money or Your Life* (Penguin Books, reissued in 2008). The authors present various formulas and exercises to help readers determine the true value of their time—or "life energy," in the authors' words—and evaluate whether you're really getting the most value out of the limited time we all have here on Earth. This classic book is credited by many cheapskates, myself included, with fundamentally reshaping their attitude toward money and life, and it was one of the most frequently recommended reference books by those responding to my questionnaire.

It's not unusual to encounter cheapskates who actually carry around a card in their wallets or purses with a homemade conversion chart on it, showing how much they earn in their jobs by the minute, hour, day, week, and so on. "It helps to put the true cost of things in perspective," one card-carrying cheapskate told me. "When I think of the joy I get out of having a day off with my kids, or reading, or relaxing, or whatever . . . *stuff* and the cost it represents in terms of my time quickly loses its appeal. It just becomes too expensive."

The cheapskate next door also recognizes that, if you go about it wrong, frugality and saving money can be a time-suck in its own right. If instead of buying that $150 pair of new boots in the department store, Clara spends two days combing yard sales and thrift stores across the city to find a used pair for only $20, then in terms of time-value she'd have been better off just buying the new pair.

That's why the cheapskate next door is a "premeditated shopper" and not a "bargain hunter," as I'll discuss in a minute. That's also why they use things up, wear things out, make things last, and, sometimes, simply do without. For the cheapskate next door, it's really more about stretching their time than it is about stretching their dollars.

3. A Cheapskate Values Value

"Frank's the kind of guy who knows the price of everything, but the value of nothing."

My friend Carol Martina has a knack for zingers, many of them directed toward Frank, her husband of forty years and a retired U.S. government accountant. "Frank's so tight, he squeaks when he walks. When he opens up his wallet, Washington and Lincoln squint from the shock of seeing daylight."

I like Carol and Frank a lot. While Frank may indeed be tight with a buck, if Carol is correct about him "knowing the price of everything but the value of nothing," then he really doesn't fit the profile of the typical cheapskate next door. Sorry, Frank. But keep trying.

In response to the questions I asked about which factors influence cheapskates most when they consider whether or not to buy a product, surprisingly "price" was not the top choice. "Quality/durability" was ranked as the number-one consideration, with about 95 percent of cheapskates ranking "quality/durability" and "price" as the top two considerations, in many cases ranking them both as equally important. As Warren Buffet once said, "Whether we're talking about socks or stocks, I like buying quality merchandise when it is marked down."

Coming in third was "something that will increase/maintain value," which I'll also discuss in a minute. Trailing far behind those top three were a variety of other factors, including a "healthy choice," "eco-friendly," "hand/locally made vs. mass produced," "country where made," and, in last place, "brand."

It's clear from the questionnaires and comments I received that for the cheapskate next door, "value" is defined as *Durability/Quality Divided by Price,* or D4D (Durability for Dollars), as I sometimes call it. This is reflective of the cheapskate's desire to own things that are going to last a very long time, and that perform well over the long haul without requiring expensive repairs or becoming functionally obsolete.

On this point, some of the cheapskates I've met kind of freaked me out, in a Rain Man sort of way. It's like they had an amortization calculator implanted in their brains. Rob Crabtree, for example, could instantly tell you whether one item—from a new car to a new pair of underwear—was a better value than another, based on the price and projected lifespan of each.

"When you don't live in a throwaway world—or at least you've made your own little world where you don't throw things away—then you need to do the math and figure out how much something costs based on how long it's going to last, not based on how long you're going to keep it before you throw it away," Rob told me.

(Hint from Rob "Rain Man" Crabtree: Go with boxers, even if they cost up to 20 percent more than briefs. Gotta factor in the increased risk of premature elastic failure with briefs, don't you know.)

4. Shopping Isn't a Cheapskate Sport

When people discover that I'm a cheapskate, I'm surprised at how often they say something like, "I just don't have all that time to shop for bargains." There's a common perception—a misperception, in my experience—that "cheapskate" is synonymous with "bargain hunter."

Don't get me wrong, we cheapskates like to get the best possible value for our money. So yeah, when we shop, we do our best to scope out bargains. But the difference between a cheapskate and a bargain hunter is that cheapskates generally don't like to shop. Cheapskates spend and consume less in large part because we take little or no joy in shopping—so we simply shop less—in contrast to most true bargain hunters I know.

Anecdotally, nearly all of the cheapskates I personally interviewed while writing this book made it clear that they don't view shopping as "recreation," "sport," or "therapy," as they often put it. That's not to say that they don't boast about what a good deal they got on this purchase, or how much they saved on that deal, because they frequently do (trust me). But in the case of the cheapskate next door, that's the result of being a smart but reluctant shopper, not a bargain hunter or hyper-consumer.

A number of studies and personal experiments over the years have supported the fact that the more time people spend shopping, the more they tend to buy and the more they tend to spend. As Gomer Pyle used to say, "Surprise, surprise, surprise."

As we'll see in Chapter 11, nearly 90 percent of the cheapskates I polled say they shop for groceries only once every week, if that often. That's in sharp contrast to the almost 50 percent of Americans who say they shop for groceries *three or four times* every week. And when asked how often they shop for clothing, a majority of cheapskates I polled responded twice per year or even less frequently.

Another rather surprising case in point: About 75 percent of those cheapskates polled say that they rarely or never shop at garage/yard sales, auctions, or rummage sales, often mentioning that such shopping venues encourage people to buy things they don't really need.

"I've never understood why people like to shop," cheapskate Janice Rogers told me. "To me it's a chore. Hell, I have more fun doing the laundry than going shopping. I guess [shopping's] like alcohol or drugs . . . some people are addicted to it, and to other people it's nothing."

According to the cheapskate next door, the best way to win at the sport of shopping is to simply refuse to take the field.

5. A Cheapskate Regrets Nothing

I've been waiting on the World Health Organization to issue a Pandemic Alert. It's clear to me that here in America we're in the midst of an epidemic of buyer's remorse. Maybe it hasn't spread globally yet, so that's why the WHO is holding off on the alert.

I recently heard a report on the NBC *Nightly News* claiming that Americans express at least "some regrets" about 80 percent of the discretionary items they buy, within one year of having made the purchase. In fairness, that's not saying that they "entirely regret" the purchase or that they'd choose otherwise if they had it to do over again. And that's just their level of regret within the *first year* of purchasing an item; I assume that the ICKM4BT (I-Could-Kick-Myself-For-Buying-That) Level steadily increases with time.

While I continue to work tirelessly in the Ultimate Cheapskate Lab to develop a vaccine to prevent buyer's remorse, results may be many years away. But there's encouraging news for all those who suffer from ICKM4BT: I've discovered that the cheapskate next door is naturally immune. Some type of anti-buying antibody, I assume.

In response to the question "On a scale of one to ten, with one being *never* and ten being *all of the time*, how frequently do you buy

an item that you eventually regret buying (aka 'buyer's remorse')
or that disappoints you?," more than 90 percent of cheapskates responded "one" (*never*). A pretty stark contrast to the NBC News report, wouldn't you say?

Evelyn "Bible Babe" Edgett confessed that she's somewhat
more susceptible to buyer's remorse than most cheapskates (she
rated herself a "three"), but told me, "When I do feel that I have
been ripped off, there's hell to pay for the guy who did it. I almost
always get my money back or a better product." Evelyn is a home-
steader way back in the hills of eastern Oklahoma. She cuts her
own firewood and slaughters her own hogs, so if you work at one
of the stores where she shops, you might want to be careful.

The cheapskate's ability to avoid buyer's remorse goes beyond
mere strategy. It's almost as if they have a sixth sense that tells
them what's a "good deal" or a "fair price," or that alerts them to a
potential purchase that they'll regret later. This makes frugality
second nature to the cheapskate next door, a simple, painless exercise. Spending less and spending smart is, for the cheapskate next
door, the path of least resistance.

It's occurred to me that this sixth sense is grounded in the
cheapskate's feelings of self-worth and self-confidence. Not spending money on things you'll regret later is as much a matter of
knowing yourself, and being comfortable with who you are, as it is
knowing who in town has the best price on blue jeans or how
highly *Consumer Reports* rates various refrigerators.

6. A Cheapskate Appreciates Appreciation (and Depreciation, Too)

At first it didn't strike me as noteworthy that most of the Amish
families I met while I was writing this book lived in homes that were

furnished with antiques. After all, if you have a horse and buggy parked in the driveway, I'd imagine that your home-decorating tastes tend toward pre–twentieth century.

I'd also assumed that the antique pieces in their homes were old family heirlooms. Great-great-grandpa Zebulon probably bought that pie safe brand-new in 1810, impressing the neighbors with the latest technological marvel when he brought it home from the store. And now it stands in the dining room of the present genera- tion of Yoders, a sort of testament to the fact that the technology clock stopped running for the Amish the day Zebulon brought that newfangled contraption into the house.

But yet again I was wrong about the Amish. It happened so often to me in my travels that I termed it "AAA"—Another Amish Ambush.

While many of the antiques I saw in the Amish homes I visited had in fact been in the family for generations, I learned that the Amish are also known for aggressively buying up antiques at estate auctions and other public sales. To my surprise, their passion for owning antiques often seemed less a matter of personal taste (i.e., wanting to look Lincoln-era chic) than it was a matter of wanting to own something that would likely retain its value or even appre- ciate in value.

Amish or not, when the cheapskates next door shop for things like furniture, homes, automobiles, and even clothing, they tend to approach it as an exercise in *acquiring assets* rather than simply *buy- ing disposable commodities*. As mentioned earlier, "something that will increase/maintain value" was ranked, after "quality/durability" and "price," as the third most important factor that influences the cheapskate's buying decisions.

That's not to say that all cheapskates buy only antique furni- ture, or that everything cheapskates buy increases in value. But other than when buying a home, how many American consumers even think about this issue of the appreciation or depreciation of most things they buy? This is a fundamental difference in the financial mindset of the cheapskate next door.

When cheapskates shop for things they need, they're ideally looking to buy things that will increase in value. Second best is buying something that will retain its value. For example, one cheapskate told me the story of a used automobile he purchased at a very good price, drove for three years himself, and then turned around and sold for exactly what he'd paid for it—in inflation-adjusted dollars.

If it's not possible to buy something that will increase or retain its value, then the last resort is to buy something that will depreciate in value the least amount and as slowly as possible. That's why the life expectancy (aka "durability") of an item is so important to the cheapskate next door. That's also why most cheapskates frequently buy used things, rather than new.

"I absolutely hate to pay for depreciation," cheapskate Roy Webb told me. "I'm happy to let someone else pay for the value things lose as a result of being sold the first time around . . . One day they're *new*, and the next day they're *used*. Same item, but worth a whole lot less a day later." From automobiles and houses, to clothing and appliances, the cheapskate next door knows that when you buy used, you're not paying for the high cost of front-end depreciation.

7. A Cheapskate Differentiates Between Needs and Wants

I wasn't too far into the interviews and other research I did for this book before I started having flashbacks to my eighth-grade boys' health class with Coach Sacstretcher. I remember the Coach droning on about "Maslow's hierarchy of human needs," a concept I never really thought he understood, despite his talent for drawing near perfect reverse-image pyramid diagrams on the overhead projector and being able to write backward faster than he could write forward. Both were skills he proudly attributed to a gridiron head injury from his youth.

For the cheapskate next door, life is very much viewed through the lens of "needs vs. wants." It's a simple concept, but one that many Americans rarely seem to think about anymore.

"We constantly evaluate our lives . . . what we buy . . . in the context of needs versus wants. We ask ourselves, 'What's the worst thing that will happen if we don't buy this?' " cheapskate Stacey Finch told me. "That's not to say that we *only* buy what we need, but when you stop and think about it, most things people spend money on are really wants, not needs, even though we convince ourselves otherwise."

Stacey's comments echo what other cheapskates told me regarding the tendency many people have to blur the lines between needs and wants. They convince themselves that they need something when in fact they really don't, or could at least choose a less costly alternative. We have made a habit of "wantonizing" our needs.

Even Coach Sacstretcher understood that food is a basic human need. But through the process of wantonization, we expand that basic need to justify a lifestyle in which many Americans now eat more meals prepared outside the home than they cook for themselves. We *need* shelter, but we *want* it in the form of a seven-thousand-square-foot home with a swimming pool. You get my point. It's about understanding that there are many different ways to meet our true needs, and we shouldn't fool ourselves about that.

As a basic thought process, the cheapskate next door differen-
tiates between needs and wants, and recognizes that there's often a
degree of both in the purchasing decisions we make everyday. But
understanding what you *really want* can take some thought and reflection, as Julia Thomson discovered.

Julia told me: "One of the most useful ideas I was ever exposed
to was the idea that the object we wish to purchase really represents a feeling we want to have. A woman buys clothes so that she
can 'feel' attractive. We buy houses in certain neighborhoods to
'feel' secure . . . and 'feel' respected and of higher status. Once I
understood that idea, I was able to break the connection between
the object and the way I felt, which opened up a whole world of
other possibilities (for getting what I really wanted). If what I
really want is to feel attractive, perhaps I can try a new hairstyle,
combine my existing clothing in new ways, or buy used clothing at
a fraction of the price."

8. A Cheapskate Is a Premeditated Shopper

Quote-meister Franklin P. Jones is credited with saying, "A bargain
is something you can't use at a price you can't resist." But as discussed before, "cheapskates" and "bargain hunters" are two very
different creatures.

While the cheapskate next door is all in favor of rooting out
true bargains, the thought process they put into it—what I call
"premeditated shopping"—and the fact that they don't really enjoy
shopping, overrides the impulse to buy stuff they don't need just
because it's being sold at a good price.

When we cheapskates shop, we shop deliberately. Premeditated
shopping has two tenets: prior planning and delayed gratification.

Whether we're shopping for groceries, clothing, or just about
anything else, we always make a shopping list before we leave

home. And that shopping list isn't just dictated off the top of our head as we head for the store. It's usually been composed on an ongoing basis and takes into account things we already have on hand, to avoid buying things unnecessarily. Many cheapskates talk about the importance of doing a "pre-inventory" before they shop.

"If it's not on my list, I don't buy it. And I only put it on the list after I've determined that I truly need it, that I don't already have one—that I can't substitute something else for it or simply do without," one cheapskate told me. "Of course, even then, I'll usually only buy it if I can find it on sale."

Prior planning also includes research—or *due diligence, cheapskate style.* About nine out of ten of cheapskates polled say that they routinely research and comparison shop for items that cost $20 or more, most often relying on the Internet and *Consumer Reports* to facilitate that process.

But even once the cheapskate has researched and targeted an item to be purchased, he's usually in no hurry to rush out and buy it, unless it's on sale or it's a true necessity. The cheapskate next door thrives on delayed gratification, or "spending procrastination," as I call it: *Put off buying today what you can always buy tomorrow.*

Many cheapskates practice what I called in my first book a "mandatory waiting period": waiting at least a week or two between the time you see a (discretionary) item in the store, and when you go back to buy it. Very often you'll never go back to buy it, and that's a big reason why the cheapskate next door rarely suffers from buyer's remorse.

9. A Cheapskate Knows the Best Things in Life Aren't Things

I certainly wouldn't use the word "Spartan" to describe the lifestyles of any of the cheapskates I encountered while writing this book. Nor would I often use the word "lavish," although that would indeed apply to at least a few. "Comfortable?" Definitely. "Eclectic?" Frequently.

The cheapskate next door is clearly less materialistic than the average American, living by the credo *Use it up. Make it last. Do without.* That's not to say that they loathe material possessions. In fact, like earlier generations of Americans, they take pride in what possessions they do own, and that pride results in a heightened sense of stewardship and care for those possessions.

Here's the really interesting thing, though. While cheapskates don't shun material possessions, they typically place a greater value on "experiences" than they place on "stuff." Not that they necessarily spend a lot of money on those experiences, although they are far more likely to splurge on travel or some other activity than they are to spend lavishly on new stuff. In response to the question "Do you ever splurge on something when it comes to spending, and, if so, on what?," more than nine out of ten respondents said they splurge on a wide range of activities—travel, family outings, celebrations, recreational activities, social events—as opposed to material objects.

The cheapskate next door knows something that numerous social scientists have confirmed, including Ryan Howell, Ph.D., an assistant professor of psychology at San Francisco State University. Howell's research not only supports the idea that spending to create life experiences, as opposed to accumulating more possessions, makes us happier; his findings also show that the relative amount we spend on those experiences doesn't directly impact the level of happiness they provide. A $27 dinner, for example, can bring the same amount of happiness as a $400 weekend getaway.

So the important thing is not how much we spend on an experience—assuming it costs anything at all—but rather that we make the effort to have them. For that, of course, we need time. That's why, as discussed before, the cheapskate next door values his time and what he can do with it more than money and the stuff he can buy with it.

When I speak to groups about the virtues of the cheapskate lifestyle, I like to ask the adults in the audience how many birthday and holiday gifts from their childhood they remember, and how many of those gifts they still own today. The answer is usually just a couple, at most, of the countless gifts most of us were showered with when we were kids.

Then I ask them how many memories from those same special occasions they remember and cherish even more with each passing year. You can see the lightbulbs coming on. As the cheapskates next door know, possessions tend to disappoint and become less valuable over time, while experiences often retain or even increase in value with age.

10. A Cheapskate Does What He Loves for a Living

No, I'm not going to tell you that all cheapskates love their jobs. In fact, roughly 20 percent of those I polled say they "hate" their jobs most or even all of the time. For them, living below their means is often considered a path to early retirement and the day they can tell their boss to take his job and shove it.

"Every time I'm tempted to blow some cash on something I don't need, I think about our plans for early retirement and how great it's going to feel to walk away from this place," one Miser Adviser told me, referring to a job he dislikes immensely. "I've even gone as far as drafting my letter of resignation when I feel that urge to splurge. That always brings me back to my senses."

Still, it was far more common for the cheapskates I met to have a job that they're truly passionate about, but one that doesn't provide much in terms of financial compensation or other tangible benefits. In response to the question "On a scale of one to ten, with one being *I hate it all the time* and ten being *I love it all the time,* how would you describe your feeling about your current job/occupation?," more than two-thirds of the cheapskates polled responded with seven or higher. At the same time, nearly 40 percent of all respondents said that they are dissatisfied with the amount of money they currently earn, although they frequently commented that their dissatisfaction with a lower salary was more than compensated for by increased job satisfaction.

These cheapskates often have careers in the nonprofit sector or are "selfishly employed." I defined "selfish employment" in my first book as "having the financial security to pursue your interests and passions as employment without undue risk or concern over income." As a selfishly employed individual myself, when people ask me what I do for a living, I usually reply, "I just do my own thing, and sometimes somebody pays me money because of it."

Schoolteacher and author of the book *How to Survive (and Perhaps Thrive) on a Teacher's Salary* (Tate Publishing, 2007), Danny Kofke told me, "I get to do what I love because I'm frugal. I feel that I was put on Earth to teach. I love being a schoolteacher, but, better yet, I love having my wife be able to stay home with our daughters. We may not earn a large income, but we are very wealthy because we get to do what we want to in life."

Ironically, not only can living below your means be the key to being able to afford to do what you love for a living, but cheapskates often told me that—because they're happy in their jobs—they tend to be less tempted to use shopping as "therapy" or to mistake money and stuff for true happiness. "Because I have a job that fulfills me, I do not need external or materialistic things to make me feel happy and content," Danny Kofke said.

I know from firsthand experience, back when I had a "real job," that when I was unhappy with what I was doing for a living or stressed out in my job, even I, the Ultimate Cheapskate, would occasionally succumb to the temptation to spend money to try to make myself feel better. After all, if I was only doing a job for the paycheck, then what was life all about if I didn't spend that paycheck on more stuff?

11. A Cheapskate Has Spending Anxiety Disorder ("SAD"—But It Really Isn't!)

Of course it's true, as a matter of definition, that cheapskates don't like spending money. As my poooor wife has said on more than one occasion, "It takes the jaws-of-life to get my husband's wallet out of his back pocket."

But in all seriousness, the extent of the mental anguish and distress the cheapskate feels when spending money, particularly in a wasteful fashion, is a very real and interesting phenomenon. I call it Spending Anxiety Disorder, or SAD, and all true cheapskates suffer from it at least on an occasional basis. In Freudian terms, I suppose it's our "superego," an instinctual trait that's just part of who we are. It sets us apart from non-cheapskates, who often seem euphoric when they shop and spend money.

This was a favorite topic of conversation with the cheapskates I interviewed: how they feel when they spend money and, specifically, when they pay full price for something. They often described physical symptoms, like "dizziness," "light-headedness," and even "nausea," when talking about spending large sums of money or spending money unnecessarily.

"I just hate the feeling . . . just really hate it . . . it's like turning on the tap full bore and just watching it go down the drain, not being able to do anything about it," Kate Easlick told me, describing the pit she feels in her stomach when she has no choice but to pay full price for something.

It's not just money a cheapskate hates wasting. As we'll see throughout this book, the cheapskate's SAD flares up whenever any type of resource goes to waste. Numerous cheapskates told me that they can't bear to see other people—even total strangers—waste money or other resources, either.

"I just try to bite my tongue, but I really want to yell, 'Do you know how much money you're wasting on that?' " Bill Nye says about the SAD attacks he has when he watches the way most other people shop. I know the feeling and frequently don't bite my tongue. Instead I routinely assail fellow shoppers in the supermarket with my unsolicited advice on how they can save a few dollars on the items in their grocery cart. ("Security Alert: There's a cheapskate loose in aisle five!")

Early-onset SAD is very common among the cheapskates next door, and may be a condition we're born with. In response to the survey question "During your lifetime, do you think you have changed your attitude about money and purchasing behavior?," nearly 90 percent of respondents said that they had not; that they had felt similarly about money even as a child.

But it's a mistake to assume that Spending Anxiety Disorder is a bad thing. I like to think of it like an allergy. Once you know you have an allergy, obviously you try to avoid whatever it is that causes the allergic reaction. Those of us with SAD of course can't avoid spending money entirely, but we can avoid spending it wastefully and avoid wastefulness in general. How is that a bad thing?

12. A Cheapskate Is Brand Blind and Advertising Averse

"If someone wants to advertise on my body, that's fine. But they need to pay me to do it, not the other way around."

Miser Adviser Emeritus Ralph Huber has a long list of pet peeves about life in general, and spending money in particular. One of his favorite rants is about paying top dollar for the "privilege" of letting designers and companies like Tommy Hilfiger and Nike display their names on his person. Ralph doesn't place much stock in brand names, although I'm pretty sure he's serious about selling Tommy space on his butt if the price is right.

Ralph is far from alone among cheapskates when it comes to his views on brand names and product advertising. As mentioned earlier, when asked to rate various factors (e.g., "price," "quality/ durability," etc.) that influence the cheapskate's purchasing decisions, "brand" came in dead last. Because cheapskates also ranked "quality/durability" as the *most* important factor, it's fair to assume that they just aren't convinced there's a correlation between popular brands and the quality/durability of the products that bear their names.

From clothing to cars to groceries, the cheapskate next door is truly *brand blind*, evaluating products on their own merits and not being seduced by the cachet of a stylish name. In part, that's because commercial advertising apparently has little if any impact on the cheapskate next door. In response to the question "On a scale of one to ten, with one being *never* and ten being *all of the time*, how frequently do you buy a product primarily because you saw it advertised and it looked appealing?," roughly 95 percent of cheapskates responded with one or two (i.e., *never* or *almost never*).

It's not just that cheapskates aren't swayed by the estimated five thousand commercial messages each of us is bombarded with every day, but many cheapskates I spoke with are truly *advertising averse*. That is, they suspect that heavily advertised products are actually inferior, overpriced, and generally a rip-off. And the cheapskate next door realizes that the cost of advertising a product is built into the price paid by the consumer.

"It took a while for me to explain to our kids that if a company needs to advertise its products all over the place, there must either be something wrong with it or it's something that people really don't need," cheapskate Welmoed Sisson of Silver Spring, Maryland, told me. "Otherwise, why would they have to advertise it so much?" I guess that means no Home Shopping Network on the tube at the House of Sisson.

13. A Cheapskate Understands Change vs. Progress

I suspect that there's a little bit of Amish in many of the cheapskates I've met. That's not to say that when it comes to embracing new technologies, all cheapskates are stuck in the horse and buggy days. For example, about two-thirds of the cheapskates I polled do in fact own a cell phone, which puts us below the national average of roughly 80 percent, but not by all that much.

But what's striking about the cheapskate's mindset and approach to new technology, and to change in general, is that many of us grasp the concept that "change" and "progress" are not necessarily the same thing. Just because something new exists, it doesn't mean that it will make our lives better or that we must allow it into our lives. Like the Amish, we cheapskates tend to take our time and think about the pluses and minuses a new product will have on our lives before we open up our wallets.

Cheapskates also know that smart consumers don't rush out

and buy the latest techno-gadget the day it's released, even if they do decide that they want to own one. New electronic items and computer technology tend to drop dramatically in price soon after they are introduced, and not only do subsequent generations usually cost less, but they often have greater functionality and fewer operating glitches. As Elvis put it, "Only fools rush in" when it comes to buying new technology.

Sometimes it may be easier to evaluate the impact technology has on your life only *after* you've allowed it into your life. Cheapskate Beth Dillehay of Rendville, Ohio, told me about an interesting experiment she and her husband, John, have been conducting, what they call the "Lazy Luddite Theory."

As various appliances began to break down at the Dillehays' house—since that's what all appliances eventually do—Beth and John decided to resist the urge to immediately replace them. They decided to see what life would be like by removing appliances they'd always had, as those appliances gave up the ghost. It's kind of a reversal of natural selection, if you will.

"First the electric hair dryer broke," Beth told me, "and we began to let our hair air dry. Next the microwave broke, and we barely miss it. We gave our dishwasher away before it broke. Those things are silly anyway; you have to basically wash the dishes before you put them in the dishwasher!" And now the Dillehays are living life just fine without their electric clothes dryer either, which a few months ago went to the great Maytag graveyard in the sky (well, actually, to the Perry County landfill).

"If I space out the loads of laundry through the week instead of doing them all on one day, I can always use the clothesline, even in the winter," Beth said. "I'm free from the expense and find this plan so liberating! It's a passive way to get machines out of your life—just wait until they destroy themselves and then do nothing

about it." It sounds like it pays in more ways than one to be a Lazy
Luddite.

14. A Cheapskate Avoids Debtor Dementia

When the cheapskates next door talk about debt, they use some
pretty colorful language. You might think they're talking about
vampire hunting instead. They often use terms like "slay it" and
"kill it." One even told me, "You need to drive a stake through it
and send it to its grave."

Living debt-free, almost by definition, is the ultimate goal of
living below your means. If you consistently spend less than you
make, then the need to borrow money should be both temporary
and relatively rare, as opposed to the way of life it has become for
most Americans. Debt, one cheapskate told me, is like "sin" in her
family. While the rest of America has been at a credit-fueled
spending party, the cheapskates next door have been true party
poopers.

The cheapskates next door never succumbed to the wave of
"debtor dementia" that has swept across America in recent generations. I define debtor dementia as "a semidelusional state commonly triggered by assuming a home mortgage or other large
debt." It's the body's way of protecting that portion of the human
brain that deals with rational thinking. Because of the size and
scope of the transaction, the dollars involved seem like Monopoly
money and the idea that you'll ever live to see the loan paid off
seems like a fairy tale. Pretty soon, taking out a home equity loan
or racking up a few grand on a credit card you can't pay off seems
to make perfect sense.

As we'll see in later chapters, cheapskates generally support
the idea of borrowing money to buy a home (nearly 95 percent of

those polled have or have had a home mortgage), but beyond that they're truly debt resistant, even when it comes to borrowing for big-ticket items like automobiles or a college education. For example, fewer than 5 percent of those cheapskates polled carry any credit card debit (i.e., if they use a credit card, they pay the entire balance every month), and only about 2 percent have outstanding home equity loans.

And when they do borrow, the retirement of that debt in full, as quickly as possible, is an overriding priority for the cheapskate next door. More than 80 percent of those cheapskates polled who own homes reported that they have already paid off or plan to pay off their home mortgages sooner than required under the terms of the loan. That's a shocker, given that roughly half of all Americans will never—*during their lifetimes*—be entirely free of a home mortgage debt and/or debt secured against their home.

"Every minute of every day that I owe someone else money is sheer agony for me," Alice Wilson told me. "It's like I'm in prison, and the only thing I can think about is getting out as quickly as possible." Alice definitely exhibits no warning signs of debtor dementia.

15. Cheapskates, Know and Trust Thyself

Spend a little time with the cheapskates next door, and I guarantee you'll find that we're full of ourselves. But I mean that in a positive way. Cheapskates tend to have a strong sense of *self*—as in being self-reliant, self-sufficient, and self-confident, with a high degree of self-worth and self-esteem.

We like to do things for ourselves whenever possible. In response to the question "On a scale of one to ten, with one being *never* and ten being *all of the time*, how frequently do you choose to do something yourself (e.g., home repairs, your taxes, yard work, washing your car, etc.) rather than hire someone to do it for you?," approximately 95 percent of cheapskates responded with a number eight or higher (i.e., *mostly* or *all of the time*).

Cheapskate Carol McAnulty of Beulah, Michigan, is a prime example of the type of self-reliant individual I'm talking about. The fifty-nine-year-old retired member of the U.S. Air Force Band heats her home during the blustery Michigan winters with a wood stove she stokes with firewood she cuts herself . . . using a hand-saw. And that's the easy part. It's getting the wood home on her bicycle from locations sometimes many miles away that really keeps Carol fit. She says the trailer on her bicycle (which, of course, she made herself from parts found in neighbors' trash) can haul a couple of hundred pounds of wood at a time. I'd estimate that's more than twice tiny Carol's body weight.

Don't confuse the cheapskate's strong sense of self with being selfish, though. Carol is a perfect example of that as well. Like many cheapskates, she chooses to live frugally for a variety of reasons, one of which is that it allows her to help others with her time and money. She volunteers hundreds of hours each year at a local nursing home and at the public library, which she helped build with a six-figure personal contribution in memory of her beloved Darcy, a small mixed terrier whom Carol—needless to say—rescued rather than purchased.

Because of our strong sense of self, we cheapskates place a premium on personal responsibility and accountability. We view our financial affairs—and our lives in general—as something that we are ultimately responsible for and can largely control. As one cheapskate put it, referring to the financial and lifestyle choices we all make every day, "The most important economy is the one you create for yourself."

On a related point, with personal bankruptcies reaching near record levels in 2008 and roughly one in every one hundred U.S. households filing for protection in that year alone, it was striking to find that less than one-half of one percent of the cheapskates polled had ever declared bankruptcy *in their entire lives*. Even asking them the question prompted a considerable number of unsolicited editorial comments: "NO!!!," "*NEVER!*," "I'd rather die than declare bankruptcy," and, my personal favorite, "I'll sell my body first! Not that it would bring much, but if you're broke, what the hell?"

The cheapskate's heightened sense of personal responsibility and trust in herself isn't to say that she totally ignores the advice of others. When it comes to seeking financial and other advice, as we'll see in Chapter 3, the cheapskate often seeks out the advice of others, but ultimately charts her own course. As sixteenth-century French philosopher Michel de Montaigne wrote, "I listen with attention to the judgment of all men, but so far as I can remember, I have followed none but my own." Or, as my Grandpa Tex said whenever he played pinochle, "I trust everybody, but I always cut the cards myself."

16. A Cheapskate Answers to a Higher Authority

Self-proclaimed cheapskate Bob Moyers has a very important job: He's God's PR agent.

It even says so on his business cards. In fact, Bob occasionally receives e-mails from his boss, the proverbial Big Man upstairs. The One in the corner office, with a view of, well, everything and everybody, I guess.

I interviewed Bob at *his* office, in his modest home near Liberty Center, Ohio. No sooner had Bob told me the story about how

God sometimes e-mails him than the computer on his cluttered desk emitted the familiar *ping* signaling an incoming message.

Given the frequency with which I'd been ending up in Sunday church services across the country as a result of writing *Road Map*, I stiffened in my chair and looked wide-eyed over at Bob as he checked the message.

"Is it Him?" I asked, in suspense.

"No. Spam," Bob replied. He seemed a little disappointed, but maybe somewhat relieved, I thought. After all, it was Friday afternoon, and who wants to have a heavenly workload dumped on him by the boss going into the weekend?

Bob, who has devoted much of his life to creating Christian-based motivational programs and materials, was one of the first people I interviewed for this book. His decision to live below his means, he told me, was part and parcel of his religious faith. "It's all part of doing His work. Money and the material things in life are meaningless. By living modestly, I can dedicate myself and my time to serving God."

I quickly discovered in writing this book that Bob is far from unique. In fact, more than nine out of every ten cheapskates I surveyed said that their decision to live below their means really isn't about money at all; their frugality and attitude toward money are rooted in higher values or beliefs they hold.

It's not about trying to save a buck for the sake of saving a buck, or seeing who can build the biggest bank account before they die. As the marketing slogan for Hebrew National hotdogs goes, the cheapskates next door "answer to a higher authority."

But that "higher authority" or belief/value system is not always religious in nature. While about 60 percent of those polled indicated that they were modestly to extremely religious, many cited nonreligious beliefs and values for their financial convictions. These frequently included environmentalism, as well as other spiritual and ethical considerations consistent with the *live below your means* lifestyle, a cornerstone of which is having more money, time, and other resources to share with those who are less fortunate.

Bruce Jackson of Lewisburg, Pennsylvania, echoed the remarks of many cheapskates I've spoken with when he told me, "Most everyone I know personally has what I consider to be a surplus of blessings. Many others in the world do not. Good stewardship of resources requires me to use resources wisely. 'Live Simply, So That Others May Simply Live,' as Gandhi said."

Jackson lives a comfortable but modest life, relying primarily on his social security income of $667 a month to cover his basic living needs, not including medical expenses. Despite his self-imposed prohibition against tapping his savings for anything other than medical and other emergency expenses, he says that most of his estate is slated to go to charities when he dies. "The more careful I am with my money, the more can be passed on to others who really need it."

How Did You Score in the Mind Game?

Now that you've had a peek inside the mindset of the cheapskate next door, how do you stack up? Do you recognize any of these sixteen core beliefs or attitudes in yourself?

Even if you're not a natural-born cheapskate, the good news is that anyone can learn to become smart about money in the finest cheapskate tradition. Breaking the shekel shackles, living what I call a "money lite" existence, boils down to choices—the choices all of us make every day, every time we get out our wallets or open up our purses.

The remaining chapters in this book are all about those choices. And not just about choices in practical matters like where and how you shop, as important as those types of decisions are. But choices about what you value in life and what you truly want out of it. Remember, you choose the relationship you have with money each and every day, and if you're not happy with that relationship, it's never too late to change it. To quote Gandhi yet again, "If I have the belief that I can do it, I shall surely acquire the capacity to do it even if I may not have it at the beginning."

CHAPTER 2

Good Habits Are Hard to Break

"How did you go bankrupt?"
"Two ways. Gradually, then suddenly."
—Ernest Hemingway, *The Sun Also Rises*

I first met Julia and Gerald Thomson on the inaugural leg of the Tour de Cheapskate in January 2008, a six-hundred-mile bicycle trek from San Diego to Tucson via Phoenix and assorted prairie dog towns in between. The desert was beautiful that time of year and the cycling was superb, despite a saucer-sized, cattle-brand-shaped saddle sore that emerged on my backside on day six, fittingly just outside of Welton, Arizona.

The Thomsons had kindly invited me to stay with them in their pleasant home in the northern suburbs of Phoenix while I was in town promoting my book. I was anxious to meet them, as I'd learned through our e-mail exchanges that they were nearing their goal of early retirement, getting ready to check out of their careers in the financial industry while still in their early forties. The story they had to share wasn't one of getting rich through investing or high-paying jobs (both earned modest salaries through most of their careers), but rather—you guessed it—living below their means.

They also told me that they taught classes and provided financial counseling to money-troubled families at their church, so I hoped to learn from those experiences as well. Plus, they'd mentioned that they owned a hot tub—a fact that wasn't forgotten by either me or the Circle-Bar-Carbuncle brand on my butt as I bicycled through the hot Arizona sun.

They say that first impressions are important. Gerald's first impression of me nearly ended with my being spread-eagle against a police squad car in a grocery store parking lot.

I'd arrived in their neighborhood a little early, so I stopped outside the Safeway store down the street from where they lived to use the pay phone. Gerald just happened to stop at the store on his way home from work, spotted me with my bicycle talking on the pay phone, and quickly introduced himself before disappearing around the corner toward the entrance to the store.

I then heard him say, "Honey, our houseguest is here!" and a few seconds later a very friendly-looking forty-something woman came around the corner toward me, smiling pleasantly. I, of course, assumed it was Julia, and—as I'm prone to do—I rushed up to her, my arms spread inescapably wide, and proceeded to give her a big old cheapskate bear hug.

I didn't realize two things: Gerald had not been talking to Julia in person when he disappeared around the corner, but rather on his cell phone; and, two, the woman I was now forcibly embracing in the deserted parking lot of a grocery store was a total stranger who was simply coming out of the store at the wrong time. Gerald heard me say something like "Julia! So good to meet you!" and he backtracked just in time to see the poor, panic-stricken woman finally break free of my sweaty clutches and scurry off to her car.

Yep, first impressions are important, particularly if you're a houseguest. "Honey, close the blinds and hide the silver, the Ultimate Cheapskate's at the door!"

CHEAP SHOT
OUT OF SIGHT, OUT OF MIND

"In our financial lives, the savings really grew when I set it up so that our paychecks were automatically deposited, part into our checking account to cover our monthly expenses and the rest into savings," Miser Adviser Lynda Thomakos told me. "Any overtime pay, raises, etc., go right into savings, and if we find ourselves taking money out of savings to cover expenses, we find out why." Lynda confirms what most cheapskates say is one of the most important good money habits you can have: direct deposit of incoming funds and automatic bill pay for the bills you pay every month, like mortgage/rent, utilities, insurance, loan payments, etc. Most employers offer direct deposit of paychecks, and automatic bill pay can be arranged with most vendors and banks. Not only is it a free service and saves time (not to mention postage stamps and gas), but it guarantees that you'll always pay your bills on time and avoid late fees and penalties.

Savings: Variable, but with late fees on credit cards and other consumer loans averaging about $30, avoid four of those bad boys a year and you'll save $120.

Poor People (Often) Have Poor Habits

Okay, before you get your knickers in a twist about the insensitivity of the above statement, let me say that of course I recognize that many poor people in the United States and around the world are truly victims of circumstances beyond their control. To think otherwise would be truly insensitive and downright stupid.

That said, we all know or at least have heard about people who have been blessed by tremendous financial good fortune—a windfall inheritance, a lucky lottery ticket, etc.—only to squander it away and end up in the poorhouse. These are clear examples of the truth behind what cheapskate Kristan Lawson told me: "The key to wealth isn't what you earn, but rather what you spend."

What might surprise you is that when it comes to money management and smart spending, the cheapskates next door usually don't spend a lot of time thinking about it. It has become automatic.

"It's like going on a diet," Gerald Thomson told me. "I used to struggle with my weight. I'd go on a diet, lose some weight, then pretty soon I'd go back to my old way of eating and gain it all back. It wasn't until I stopped dieting and instead changed my eating and exercise habits for good that I managed to lose the weight and keep it off. Now I don't even need to think about it anymore."

Based on their own experience and those of the financially troubled folks they counsel through their church, the Thomsons, like most cheapskates I spoke with, believe that the key to smart money management is to make it effortless, second-nature, the "default setting" in your life. "People always say that bad habits are hard to break. And they are. But it's also true that good habits are just as hard to break," Gerald told me.

"We try to help the people we counsel look at their finances, especially their spending, and replace their bad habits with good habits," Julia Thomson said. She gave an example of helping people to break the bad habit of paying ATM fees at "foreign" banks. It's as simple as choosing a bank that's most convenient to where you live, work, and shop, and planning ahead by getting the cash that you need for the week when you shop for groceries and at other places that provide cash back without charging a fee.

"Sometimes it's hard to convince people to spend less—they view it as a hardship, a sacrifice," Julia says about their financial counseling experience. "But who gets any joy out of paying ATM fees? How does paying ATM fees make you any happier?"

As we'll see in Chapter 3 and throughout this book, there are many other good money habits that the cheapskates next door have built into their daily lives; everything from direct deposit of paychecks and automatic bill pay (see Cheap Shot), to never going grocery shopping without a grocery list or when they're hungry,

---

CHEAP SHOT
$100 SPENDING HABIT TO BREAK

"I don't know what I'd do without vending machines," George Hargrove told me. He sounds like a lot of Americans, since we spend nearly $30 billion every year on products dispensed by vending machines. That works out to more than $150 per American adult. But George "Loose Change" Hargrove isn't like most Americans, because he never *buys* anything from vending machines. He just stops at every one he sees to check the coin return. He even travels with a foldable yardstick he uses to retrieve coins that are hiding underneath the machines with the dust bunnies. No, I'm not suggesting that we all get out our yardsticks and encroach on George's nickel-and-dime mother lode. But products dispensed from vending machines usually cost three to ten times as much as the same products sold in stores, so vending machines are a bad habit worth breaking.

Savings: $100+ per year, but of course you may bankrupt poor George in the process.

to de-cluttering their homes at least once a year in order to avoid buying things they don't need.

It's all about making frugality the most convenient choice, the path of least resistance.

Sure, relatively small expenses like ATM fees can add up to big money over time. But when it comes to establishing good money habits, it's the principle of the thing—not the dollar amounts involved—that matters most to the cheapskate next door. By making it a point to establish good money habits regarding even the smallest expenses, the cheapskate next door knows that smart decisions regarding the major money issues and big-ticket items in life will follow naturally.

Choose Your Friends Wisely

When it comes to establishing your money management and spending habits, the other people in your life play a key role, one way or the other.

"There are two kinds of people: those who ask for separate checks and those who don't. We prefer to make friends with the former," Gerald Thomson told me. "Man," I thought to myself, "now there's a slogan that's worthy of its own T-shirt."

That sentiment was echoed time and again when I asked cheapskates about their friends and social networks. Although none admitted to selecting friends solely based on their attitudes about money, most readily offered that they felt most comfortable with and attracted to other people who shared their sense of frugality and general attitudes toward money. For most cheapskates, shared attitudes about money and, specifically, spending wisely, outweigh things like shared social class or political or religious beliefs/affiliations when it comes to who they prefer to hang out with.

"It's not just about who we socialize with," Amy Williams says. "It's also about trying, as best as we can, to encourage our kids to hang out with other kids who come from homes with similar values about materialism and money." Amy admits that this is easier said than done, but like other cheapskate parents I spoke with, she says it's the most potent way to counteract the peer pressure among kids to own the latest fashions and buy the hottest new techno-gadgets. "If your friends don't own one, there's no pressure on you to own one either," Amy says. Many cheapskate parents who homeschool their children indicated that shielding their kids from this materialistic peer pressure is a chief benefit of home schooling.

Cheapskates want friends they feel comfortable around, and not only to avoid that potentially embarrassing "separate check" issue that Gerald mentioned. They also crave the company of people they can talk with openly about money (and I'm not talking about *bragging*), and even confide in and learn from when it comes to their personal finances.

As one Miser Adviser put it: "Learn about people who live on less than you do, and hang out with them." That sounds like good advice, just so long as they don't try to stick me with the check.

Choose Your Spouse Even More Wisely

"My wife isn't too good at living within her means," John L. Hoh, Jr., from Milwaukee told me. "That's definitely something to look for when you get married. That's my 'buyer's remorse,'" he added with a smile.

Fortunately, Hoh is cheapskate enough for himself and his wife and his eight-year-old son. In fact, Hoh claims that one of his favorite money-saving strategies is to scour after-Christmas sales for discounted apparel and other holiday items that feature Santa and the familiar "HoHoHo." "You see, they're not only cheap, but for our family they're already monogrammed," he says, referring to his last name. This guy's a genius in my book.

Like most cheapskates, Hoh has been married only once. "Isn't that enough?" he jokes. Of the cheapskates surveyed, only about 25 percent of their marriages have ended in divorce, roughly half the national average. This does not suggest that cheapskates are too cheap to get divorced, but it is worth noting that choosing the right life partner and staying together is one of the smartest financial moves you can make in your life. According to divorcesupport .com, marrying and then divorcing can easily reduce your standard of living by half to two-thirds or more, with similar consequences for the net worth amassed over your lifetime.

While having like-minded attitudes and expectations about money is of course a good idea in any marriage—whether you're married to a cheapskate or a spendthrift—Hoh's experience of being happily (albeit sarcastically) married to someone who doesn't share all of his frugal ideals isn't that uncommon among the cheapskates I spoke with. Often, one partner was considered the "cheapskate" in the relationship, and it was as frequently a man as a woman.

The secret to reconciling the differing approaches to money is clearly the two c's, *communication* and *compromise*. Danny Kofke and his wife make it a point to sit down and chat about their finances once every week. And even Gerald and Julia Thomson, who largely see eye to eye when it comes to money, set up a special discretionary fund for Julia's occasional splurges that she thinks would bother Gerald if they were paid for out of "joint funds." Not surprisingly, now that she knows that the funds are there and she can spend them without feeling guilty, Julia finds that her sense of fi-

CHEAP SHOT
FISCAL FASTING: SPENDING DETOX TO HELP BREAK BAD HABITS

I wrote extensively in my first book about the practice I call "fiscal fasting": going for a week every year without spending *any* money. Having practiced this financial ritual my whole adult life, I wasn't prepared for the reaction I got to this simple proposition from readers and the media. When Matt Lauer first interviewed me about it on *Today*, his demeanor suggested that I must be joking; apparently Matt couldn't fathom holstering his ATM card for even a single day. But then I began to hear from folks from across the country who were actually trying it. They told me things like: "I couldn't believe how much food we already had in our cupboards." "I never knew that there was a carpool from our neighborhood to within two blocks of my office." "Did you know that you can borrow movies from the library for free?" A fiscal fast will do three things: 1) You'll save some money that week by using up things you already have on hand and, in some cases, by doing without (heresy, I know!); 2) You'll break bad spending habits and gain new insight into how you spend—and probably waste—money during a typical week; 3) You'll be reminded of how many terrific things in life don't require the spending of money.

Savings: The typical American family of four spends about $320 per week just on food, clothing, transportation, and entertainment.

nancial frustration is gone and she rarely feels compelled to spend the money that's been set aside.

"I've actually only made one purchase that Gerald didn't initially approve of, and that was our hot tub," Julia told me. "But now he loves it!" Given that I was soaking my road-weary bones in the Thomsons' hot tub as she told me this, I was instantly convinced that setting up such a special discretionary fund can be a brilliant financial move in many marriages.

And all of these interactions with other couples reassured me that my own blissfully-happy-yet-sometimes-financially-lopsided marriage of twenty-six years isn't a fluke. Although, just the other day, my pooooor wife complained, "Jeff, can't we at least once go out to dinner and a movie without having to stop at the blood bank first?" Yet again, *c'est la cheapskate.*

CHAPTER 3

Money Management, Cheapskate Style

**The time to save is now. When a dog gets a bone
he doesn't go out and make a down payment
on a bigger bone. He buries the one he's got.**
—Will Rogers

The best way to double your money these days is to fold it in half and put it back in your wallet." That's a little cheapskate humor, a line I heard a lot more than once as I traveled the country to pick the brains of my fellow cheapskates during the worst economic downturn since the Great Depression.

I can't claim that the cheapskates next door have been immune to the economic downturn, and they're clearly concerned about it just like everybody else. Like so many other Americans, some have lost jobs and most have seen their retirement and other savings decline or even plummet.

But what's striking is that, because of the way the cheapskates next door were living prior to the recession, their lives have changed relatively little, if at all, as the economy has imploded around them. Because they've consistently lived below their means—and because they've been burying their bones all along rather than making down payments on bigger bones—they're able to thrive as they always have, even when times are tough.

The good news is it's not too late to learn from them and to start managing your money *cheapskate style*.

The Spending Autopsy

"I just couldn't stand it if I had to live within a strict budget." That's the reaction you often get from people when they learn that you're a cheapskate. And I feel exactly the same way.

The reality is that my wife and I don't have a household budget, strict or otherwise. We've never had a budget in our twenty-six years of marriage. What's more, we're the rule, not the exception, among the cheapskates next door.

Contrary to what most non-cheapskates seem to think, only about 10 percent of the cheapskates polled said that they have a formal, written household budget. For most of us, a budget seems too much like a diet: a plan that's always looming over you, bringing you down, when what you really need is a lasting lifestyle change that makes the desired behavior effortless.

While we're not big fans of budgets, the cheapskates next door do place a high priority on *keeping score*, doing at least an occasional reality check to see how they're actually spending their money. It's what I call a *spending autopsy*. Approximately 85 percent of the cheapskates surveyed say that they track their spending either on an ongoing basis or periodically (e.g., a month or two out of every year). David and Caroline Llewellyn of Euless, Texas, are pretty typical in this regard, tracking their expenses against their average monthly income (after taxes) for one or two months out of every year, in order to provide a "spending template" for the other months.

Most cheapskates rely on an old-fashioned pocket journal and a newfangled computer program, like Quicken or Microsoft Money, to perform an autopsy of their spending. The pocket journal, of course, is carried on your person at all times to record cash and other spending transactions as they occur (i.e., how much you spend, when, where, and on what). That running tally is then combined with other spending records that might not be included in your pocket journal, like some check or credit card transactions, or bills that are automatically deducted out of your checking account or paycheck.

Then, depending on how complicated you want to make it, that data is sometimes entered into a computer program so you can manipulate it into different spending categories, display it in the form of colorful pie charts, and otherwise amuse and amaze yourself.

Another increasingly popular approach among cheapskates looking to simplify their spending autopsies and earn cash back or other perks (see Chapter 15) is to use a credit card and/or debit card for all purchases whenever possible. Of course, being cheapskates, they pay off the whole card balance every month to avoid interest charges, but in exchange they do get nifty account statements from companies like American Express that make it easy to categorize and review your spending.

Cheapskate Lynda Thomakos writes: "If you think you can trust yourself to not spend more because of it, I highly recommend stickin' it to the banks by using cash-back credit cards for everything you can and paying the balance every month (through an automatic payment plan). It's fun having our credit cards only *making* us money. It also makes it very easy to see where every nickel is being spent when it's almost all on the credit card statement. Hubby says it makes balancing the checkbook easier too."

Personally, I don't do any of that computer stuff, and I try to avoid using credit cards as much as possible. (For one thing, I know merchants are paying the bank fees for every credit card transaction, and I'd rather help out local business owners by paying cash.) So my "spending autopsy" strategy is just to sit down twice a year with my pocket journal (which, like the Llewellyns, I use only to record expenses during two "test months" out of the year) and other spending records for those months, and I analyze the raw data directly, albeit with a calculator (and cold beer) at my side. I guess you could say I'm a traditionalist, or maybe a minimalist, when it comes to my own spending autopsies.

I'm mostly looking for red flags—expenses that seem high, either higher than I remember them being in the past or higher than I'd like them to be. These are the things I'll dig into further or try to control more carefully going forward; they're also sometimes things that I'll "chat" with my poooor wife about, if she's the spender in question.

"But isn't the patient already dead?" you might be thinking. "What's the point of doing an autopsy, of analyzing the money you've already spent?" According to the Llewellyns, an occasional spending autopsy "will give you an idea of what items can be eliminated from your monthly expenses to help in adding to your savings and retirement accounts or paying off debt."

The point is to learn from your mistakes and to take a moment, as cheapskate Emma Schmitz told me, "to ask yourself, 'Is it really worth it? Is this really how I want to spend my money and the time that it represents?'" For example, you might discover that you're spending more on fast food than you're spending on groceries, and start to question the lifestyle implications behind those spending choices. Or, as one cheapskate was shocked to learn, she was spending more on gas, clothing, and lunches out in conjunction with her part-time job than she was making from the job!

A spending autopsy is also a chance to really drill into the rou-

tine "fixed costs" most of us pay every month without even thinking about them, things like utilities, phone, and insurance. Most
cheapskates review each of these fixed costs at least once or twice
a year. Try it, and you may be surprised to find that they are not as
"fixed" as you might assume. It's usually well worth your time to
call each of your fixed-cost vendors at least once a year to review
your current services/program and ask them, point blank, if they
can help you lower your monthly bill (see Chapter 9). It's also
worth spending an hour or two online at the same time checking
out their competitors and other alternatives.

A spending autopsy is a way of modifying your future spending—and lifestyle—based on your actual and evolving behavior.
It's not a time-consuming, abstract exercise like putting together
a detailed household budget, which too often turns into a plan of
inaction.

Spending Less Than Your Age: The New Measure of Success?

I realize that it's now an outdated concept, but thirty years ago
when I graduated from college, "earning your age" was the gold
standard for measuring whether you were financially successful in
your chosen career. For example, if you were pulling down at least
$30,000 a year by the time you were thirty years old, then you were
doing well for yourself and could attend your high school class re-
union with your nose pointed upward.

Like any rule of thumb, even back then it was too general to
apply across the board. Having spent my whole career working in
nonprofit organizations, it was a good many years before I started
earning anywhere close to my age. I probably caught up to that
standard just about the day it became obsolete and the bar was

raised even higher. In fact, to be successful by that measure, I would have needed to earn more than double the $10,000 salary I received in my first nonprofit job . . . or else still be in the fourth grade. Fortunately, I've never had any interest in attending my class reunions.

And so I'm somewhat reluctant to propose a new measure of personal financial success for this new economy we're living in, knowing that it, too, can't possibly apply to everyone. But the interesting thing about the new standard for success I'm proposing— *spend less than your age*—is that spending is nearly always more controllable than earning. This is a standard that a great many Americans should be able to achieve, because the vast majority of the time *we* control our spending. Even when we neglect it or try to abdicate our responsibility, those are choices, too.

The idea of spending less than your age grew out of my own experience and was ratified by the real-life experiences of the cheapskates next door. In a great many cases, it was consistent with their financial profiles in the first halves of their lives. (Later in life, of course, they tend to spend a fraction of their age.) It also makes some sense when you look at national income statistics. According to the U.S. Census Bureau, the median annual household income in 2007 was $50,233, and the median earnings for someone employed full time was $40,107. Since the median age of adults currently in the U.S. workforce is forty-one years of age, spending less than your age would mean spending less than you earn, a bedrock principle of cheapskate finance.

In their college and young adult years, cheapskate offspring usually spend far less than their age. That's in sharp contrast to so many college students and young adults who go away to prestigious schools, drive new cars, rack up credit card charges, and rely either on Mom and Dad or on student loans or other borrowing to spend as if they're already middle-aged. By the time they're actually middle-aged, often they're so far in debt and living so far beyond their means that in "money years" they're ready for the nursing home!

Here's an example of what I'm talking about. I met cheapskate Kelly Kamann at a book talk I gave at a small library outside of Toledo on the Ohio leg of the Tour de Cheapskate. She was in the audience that evening. Well, actually, she and a friend of hers *were* the audience that evening. The good thing about a small turnout at an event like that (if two people qualifies as a "turnout" at all) is that you can just sit down and talk to the folks who came out to hear you, rather than talk at them.

Kelly immediately struck me as a young woman who has her financial act together. She was in her late twenties, single, and working as an occupational therapist with a United Way nonprofit agency, a job she was clearly passionate about. Kelly's a prime example of a cheapskate whose frugality allows her to do what she loves for a living—and help many others through her work—even though the remuneration is relatively modest.

Kelly paid her own way through college, although she did take out a $16,000 student loan, which she repaid within four years of graduation. Now she's entirely debt-free, except for the mortgage on the small (1,000 square feet) but very charming home she's buying. Being a cheapskate, she's paying a little extra every month to retire that mortgage early. She drives a nice car (fully paid for), dresses very attractively, and vacations in Europe and elsewhere about once a year.

Kelly is now fortunate to be "earning more than her age," although not by a huge amount. Given the whopping 25 percent of every paycheck she socks away in savings (including her retirement account) and the generous amounts she gives to charity, Kelly is a living example of how—even at a young age, when you're just starting out and money is tight—you can live a very good life by "spending less than your age," or at least close to it.

The Cheapskate's Take on Saving

There's a time-tested saying in the carpentry trade: *Measure twice, cut once.* If you've ever cut a board too short, you know the wisdom of that one.

Cheapskates Daniel Newman and Bruce Ostyn shared with me a similar-sounding—and similarly wise—approach to saving for big-ticket items and splurges: *Save twice, spend once.* Whenever possible, the pair tries to save twice or even three times the amount they'll need to buy something before they take the plunge and make the purchase. It's a way of making sure they really want it, and, Daniel told me, "That way we don't feel like we are broke after we make the purchase, and we are less likely to feel remorse."

This *save twice, spend once* savings strategy relates back to an experience Bruce had when he was growing up. Once he was old enough to hold down a job, and still living with his parents, Bruce was required to turn over half of everything he earned to his father. At the time, Bruce understood that the money was to help cover his share of household expenses. While he didn't much like it, he never questioned his father about it.

Much to Bruce's surprise, on the day he moved out of his parents' home, his father handed him a check for the entire amount he'd been commandeering from Bruce's paychecks, plus interest. "It's something I'll never forget . . . It's a lesson that's been with me my whole life," Bruce told me. For Bruce, the lesson he learned was that saving, like money itself, is all relative. When his father handed over that check, Bruce realized that he hadn't really missed the money his father was secretly setting aside for him, and he knew that if he'd had it to spend, it would all be gone. That epiphany—that it's possible to set aside savings without feeling like you're sacrificing—led to Bruce's *save twice, spend once* strategy being second-nature at this point in his life.

Emergency Funds: Another Eye-Opener

So much has been written in recent years about the importance of having a designated "emergency fund" that I was fairly shocked to find that fewer than 20 percent of the cheapskates I polled have a formal emergency fund set aside. At the same time, I was rather comforted by that finding, because I've never had an official emergency fund myself. It doesn't mean that 80 percent of the cheapskates next door are ill-prepared for a financial emergency; far from it. We just see things a little differently and plan accordingly.

As you've probably heard, many personal finance pundits recommend that you have an emergency fund of three to six months' worth of living expenses set aside in a savings or other ready-access account in case you lose a job or encounter some other financial upheaval. With the recent downturn in the economy, some are now suggesting that you should index the amount in your emergency fund against the rising unemployment rate. For example, if the unemployment rate is 8 percent, you should have eight months' worth of living expenses in your emergency fund. To me it sounds more like morning talk show fodder than rational financial planning.

In part it's just a difference in semantics: All but a handful of the cheapskates polled reported that they have some funds available in cash or short-term investments that could be accessed quickly, and without penalty, if they encounter an unexpected financial emergency of some kind—even though they don't consider this to be an "emergency fund" per se. Such funds often consist of one or more "pots of money," as cheapskates are fond of calling them, that are being accumulated for a specific purpose (as I'll discuss in a minute), but could be tapped for more immediate emergency purposes if necessary.

The lack of a formal emergency fund seems to grow out of the cheapskate's unique attitude toward "emergencies." "An emergency is any situation you failed to plan for," cheapskate and retired army sergeant Bob Haas told me. "Setting aside some general money for a general emergency isn't necessarily a bad thing to do, but it's more important for people who don't live responsibly in the first place. Most people don't plan for anything. They go along, everyday . . . make foolish decisions . . . then the slightest thing happens and they're in trouble. God forbid that they lose a job or have an accident or something truly awful happens. That's when their paycheck-to-paycheck lifestyle crashes apart."

According to Bob and other cheapskates I spoke with, the need for a formal emergency fund lessens when you consistently live below your means and, even more important, live debt-free or close to it. One cheapskate said, "A financial planner once told me that I should have six months' salary on hand to cover my expenses if I lost my job. When I told him how little money I live on—and I have no debts, not even a mortgage—he agreed that one month's salary should be more than sufficient."

That's the beauty of living below your means.

Sinking Funds . . . to Avoid That Sinking Feeling

While the cheapskates next door may not have an emergency fund per se, they often establish one or more separate accounts in which

CHEAP SHOT
EXTENDED *DISSERVICE* PLANS

So-called "extended service plans" or "extended warranties" sold by many stores for consumer electronics, appliances, and other items are a *great deal*—for the store selling them and for the salesperson, who usually makes a refrigerator-sized commission on every one sold. For example, according to an article in the *Minneapolis Star Tribune*, in 2007 more than half of Best Buy's profits came from the sale of extended warranties—more than the profits from the sale of the merchandise itself! Now that should tell you something. No matter how wise they sound when the salesman explains them, in real life these types of plans don't pay off for the vast majority of consumers who buy them. Either the item doesn't need to be repaired or replaced during the window of time covered by the extended plan, or it does and we've forgotten that we bought the extra coverage in the first place. And remember, manufacturer warranties are usually included in the purchase price and provide for repair/replacement on the front end of owning a product, when a defect is most likely to show up. The cheapskates next door skip these extended disservice plans, which typically cost 10 to 20 percent of the product's purchase price, or even more.

Savings: Variable, but an extended warranty on a $900 plasma screen TV at Best Buy currently costs about $170 (now *that's* a lot of pints of plasma—see the next Cheap Shot).

they accumulate savings on a regular basis to cover a specific future liability (like out-of-pocket costs not covered by insurance—see Chapter 14), or to ensure that they will have adequate funds on hand to cover the replacement of a specific item (like an automobile—see Chapter 12) that has a limited and fairly predictable lifespan.

Borrowing terminology from the corporate and real estate worlds, you might say cheapskates are fans of so-called "sinking funds," preferring these designated "pots of money" over a general "emergency fund." Again, part of it is just a difference in semantics, but it's also a reflection of cheapskates' financial preparedness and feeling that they are responsible for "creating their own economy."

Sinking funds can be as simple as the pickle jar Jane Jesse keeps on top of her washing machine for depositing loose change and occasional cash harvested from pants pockets before doing the wash; the proceeds stored in the pickle jar are specifically designated to replace the washer or dryer when it gives up the ghost. Old-fashioned Christmas savings clubs offered by banks are another simple form of sinking fund, as is a certificate of deposit you purchase to fund a future obligation like a child's wedding, or more complicated savings programs like 529 college savings plans. Bottom line: Planning ahead is a hallmark of cheapskate money management.

Start Young and Set It on Autopilot

When it comes to savings plans, the cheapskates next door say *make it a lifelong practice, and make it automatic.*

Cheapskates start setting aside a portion of their earnings as savings from almost the very first dollar they earn in life. And, as we'll see in Chapter 4, they encourage—or even insist—that their children do the same.

Even as young adults, when money is tight, cheapskates striking out on their own continue to put away something, even if it's a minimal amount. A number of twenty-something cheapskates told me that they've set up plans with their banks so that every week or

---

CHEAP SHOT
SELL YOUR BLOOD INSTEAD

No, not really . . . although it does help save lives and plasma donors typically earn about $20 per biweekly visit (see BloodBanker.com). What I'm talking about is doing anything and everything possible to avoid the biggest bloodsucking rip-offs out there when it comes to consumer borrowing. The cheapskates next door will eat nothing but ramen noodles for a year before they'll even think about taking out any of these loans: PAYDAY LOANS—Borrow against your next paycheck at an annual interest rate that's often 400 percent or higher, and that's *before* "renewal fees" and other add-ons; CREDIT CARD CASH ADVANCES—As if the interest on credit card purchases isn't bad enough, interest on cash advances is usually much higher, averaging about 22 percent, plus an additional up-front fee of as much as 5 percent; CAR TITLE LOANS—If you own a car outright, you can borrow about 55 percent of its value—at an annual interest rate of around 300 percent, plus hefty monthly renewal fees. Default, and the lender takes your wheels. [*Note to Self: Anything money-related that's advertised on daytime TV probably isn't a good deal.*]

Savings: Variable, but a $1,000 payday loan carried for a month will probably cost you about **$225** in interest and fees—what a deal!

two, ten or twenty dollars is automatically transferred from their checking account into their savings account. "Even though I'm stretched," one twenty-four-year-old cheapskate told me, "I can always find a way to get by without that extra ten dollars each week in my checking account. In a year I'll have $500 plus interest in my savings account, then I'll be lovin' my life."

By the time they're in their thirties, most of the cheapskates polled are contributing the maximum allowable amount to employer-sponsored retirement plans. As they age, they begin saving for specific goals (e.g., buying a house, having children, starting a business), investing in a variety of ways, as we'll see in a minute, but usually doing so by setting up an automatic savings plan, either through payroll deductions or authorized bank transfers.

"Out of sight, out of mind," one cheapskate told me about the system he set up to have money from every paycheck automatically deposited into four or five different investment and savings accounts, each designated for a different long-term goal. "I can't trust myself, so I let the bank do it for me."

Not surprisingly, the cheapskate next door tends to prefer a relatively conservative investment strategy. (Contrary to urban myth, I've yet to find a cheapskate who has money buried in the backyard or stuffed in a mattress, although, given the recent investment climate, that's clearly where the smart money would have been.) Of cheapskate portfolios I was made privy to, the key characteristics were these:

- **Diversification** with a large percentage of bonds and other lending investments, and a smaller share of equities than is typically promoted in the financial media.
- **Minimizing fees,** particularly by investing in index mutual funds or "exchange-traded funds," which are so-called "bas-

kets" of related securities designed to track existing indexes like the S&P 500.

- **Rebalancing** investments periodically, according to an asset allocation plan.
- **Dollar-cost averaging**, or, in other words, continually investing on a regular schedule to even out fluctuations in the markets.
- **Remembering that "pigs get fat, hogs get slaughtered"** (as one cheapskate put it). Cheapskates don't get too greedy or aggressive, because it's only money, and the cheapskate next door doesn't need that much of it to be truly happy.

The Cheapskate's Take on Credit and Debt

The cheapskate's credit history is, by today's standards, not much of a history at all. A typical profile of the cheapskate's credit history might look strikingly similar to that of an average American living forty or fifty years ago. What's noteworthy is not what it includes, but what it *doesn't* include.

"Everybody's talking about their credit score these days. I couldn't give a flying fig what my credit score is!" cheapskate Greg Baumhart told me. "Credit scores are only important to people who need credit, and, thank you sir, that ain't me."

While I would argue that, regardless of your position on borrowing money, monitoring your credit is a prudent thing to do (do it for free at AnnualCreditReport.com), Baumhart and his "flying fig" comment captures the passion the cheapskate next door feels when it comes to debit and credit.

The cheapskate's credit history probably looks more like your great-grandfather's credit history than your own. At every juncture where today we're encouraged to borrow money to *get what we want, right now*, cheapskates resist. They either refuse to borrow entirely, or, when they do take on credit, they borrow as little as possible and pay it off as quickly as possible.

Consider the points in most people's lives at which they borrow money, or at least consider borrowing. In general, here's how the cheapskates next door are different:

- They don't borrow money to buy their first car while in high school (Chapter 12). They'll either do without a car of their own or save up whatever they can and pay cash for a used one.
- They don't run up credit card debt—*ever*—let alone while they still have acne. A 2005 report by Nellie Mae, the student lender, found that 76 percent of college undergraduates had credit cards, with an average balance of $2,169. That's a good start toward adulthood, because the average American household has about nine credit cards and credit card debt of nearly $10,000. The cheapskates next door have about 1.2 credit cards on average, and more than 90 percent of them pay off their balances in full, every month.
- They frequently don't take out student loans to finance their college educations (Chapter 4), or they borrow the absolute minimum amount possible and pay it off before even thinking about borrowing for anything else after college.
- They will take out a mortgage to buy a home, but usually buy a more modest home than they could qualify for, stay in it a good long time, and pay off their mortgage early (Chapter 10).
- And what about second mortgages, home equity loans, lines of credit, reverse mortgages, payday loans, etc., etc., etc., to pay for home remodeling, the kid's college, a summer cottage, retirement, a European vacation, etc., etc., etc.? Get outa here! The cheapskates next door couldn't give a flying fig about any of those "loan instruments." As John "Doc" Dochnahl

told me, "If you can't afford to pay for it now, you can't afford it."

How do they do it? How do the cheapskates next door avoid the pitfalls of debt that ensnare so many Americans from such a young age?

Well, that's really the whole story of this book, but in short it's a pretty simple two-part strategy. As we'll see time and again, cheapskates take a nontraditional approach to the big-ticket items in life, and—just as important—they creatively control their spending on a wide range of small-ticket items. That's the one-two punch that gives the cheapskates next door the freedom from debt that so few Americans enjoy, and is one of the reasons why they live so happily.

Admittedly, the cheapskates next door know far more about how to *stay* out of debt than they do about how to *get* out of debt. Relatively few of those I spoke with or polled had ever had large amounts of unsecured debt, either as a result of choice or conditions beyond their control (e.g., medical emergencies, etc.). When asked for advice they could offer others on how to get out of debt, the most common response was something akin to "Don't get into debt in the first place."

But cheapskate Becky Conroy has unfortunately had some firsthand experience when it comes to digging out from under the burden of personal debt. Just about the very day Becky was diagnosed with breast cancer, her twenty-four-year-old daughter, Sarah, revealed that she was on the verge of being evicted from her apartment and having her car repossessed, and that she had racked up more than $13,000 in credit card debt that she couldn't begin to pay. Talk about a bad day.

"I know it sounds whacky . . . . I was facing a possible death sentence . . . but in my mind, both situations were exactly the same," Becky said. "Neither one (cancer/debt) was going to go away on its own, only get worse. It wasn't like you could wake up the next day and say, 'I have more important things to do today than to deal with that.' The walls were closing in . . . there was that priority, staring you in the face."

Drastic situations call for drastic action, and for the cheapskate next door being in debt is a drastic situation, almost as much as a life-threatening illness. In Becky's case, an immediate, aggressive medical protocol has, thankfully, sent her cancer into remission and saved her life. Paralleling that, Becky and her husband worked with Sarah on an equally immediate, aggressive plan to help her dig her way out of debt. "It wasn't fun . . . or nearly as easy as going into debt," Sarah says, "but when I saw what Mom was going through, it put my problems in perspective and I thought, damn it, if she can whip hers, then I can whip mine."

Sarah was able to sublet her apartment through the end of her lease and move back home with her parents, which was comforting and helpful to Becky and the rest of the family during their time of need. She then sold her car to a friend who generously agreed to pay her what she still owed on it. Sarah now shares a ride to work with her father or coworkers, depending on their schedules, and is setting aside a small amount from every paycheck to buy an inexpensive used car in a few months.

Her credit card debt is headed in the right direction—downward—but she's still working on it. Sarah sold a couple of pieces of furniture she owned and started working every other weekend to generate extra funds, 100 percent of which went directly to her credit card debt. She was able to consolidate some of the debt from her higher-interest-rate cards onto a card with a lower interest rate, and then she began "snowballing" the payments.

"Snowballing" is a term used by personal finance guru Dave

Ramsey. It means that you make the minimum payment on all of your credit cards, except the one with the highest interest rate; that's the one you focus on paying off first, paying just as much

CHEAP SHOT
STRETCHING YOUR CHARITABLE DONATIONS

When it comes to charitable giving, the Joneses had better be worried about keeping up with the cheapskates next door: On average, the cheapskates polled say that they give nearly *5 percent* of their income to charities (including religious institutions), which is well above the national average of less than 3 percent. But, as with everything in life, the cheapskates want to get the most bang for their buck. That's why they check out charities first (at charitynavigator.org) to make sure they're legit and see how wisely they spend their money. Many employers will also match your charitable gifts, dollar for dollar up to a specified limit, allowing you to double your support for the qualifying charity of your choice. Or, if your employer doesn't have a matching gift program, challenge your friends and family to match your donations to a mutually acceptable charity. Miser Adviser Al Levine of Roswell, Georgia, has raised more than $76,000 through fundraising events he's organized and underwritten over the past nineteen years.

Savings: Double your contributions to charity through an employer or friend/family match, and add another **$1,000** to the grand that the typical U.S. household already contributes to charity each year.

extra on it as you possibly can each month. Once that credit card has been paid off, you take the same approach to the card with the next highest interest rate, and so on down the line. Each time you pay off a card, you have that much more money every month to put toward paying off the next card, thus the "snowball" effect.

Sarah says that getting the debt off her back is giving her a tremendous sense of newfound freedom, but the biggest challenge is changing her lifestyle so that she'll never end up in the same situation again. "What scares me is how easy it was (getting into debt) . . . and how clueless I was about money back then," she says.

Sarah's had to make changes in many areas, such as who she hangs out with and what she does with her free time. To keep herself motivated, she carries two things in her purse at all times: the letter from her previous landlord threatening eviction, and a picture of her mom taken the day she came home from the hospital.

Sarah says that once her credit cards are entirely paid off, she'll keep only one card—for bona fide emergencies—and the next and only time in her life that she ever plans to borrow money will be to someday buy a house of her own. "As Mom always says, 'If you don't have a good time, you usually have a good experience,' and that pretty much sums up what we've both been through."

CHAPTER 4

The Oxygen Mask Approach to Raising Kids

A happy childhood is the worst possible preparation for life.
—Kinky Friedman

Make no mistake about it: The cheapskates next door love their kids with all their hearts.

That's been abundantly clear in each and every cheapskate home I've ever visited. Time and again I've seen it reflected in ways you just can't fake; in the nuances of inside jokes, in smiles of mutual adoration, in the beam of a truly proud parent. It's so heartwarming and genuine that I sometimes thought I'd walked into a rerun of *The Waltons*.

Is that why, as I met more and more cheapskate families, I kept having flashes of déjà vu? Eventually I realized that what I was being reminded of was not John Boy, but my own childhood, a not at all unpleasant experience, but definitely a simpler, less materialistic upbringing than most kids have today. It was not, as the saying goes, a childhood in which much was served to you on a silver platter.

The kids of cheapskates—virtually every last child I met—impressed me immensely. Not having children of my own, I try not to judge other people as parents, but all I can say is that the cheapskate parents I met are definitely doing something right. Their kids seemed extremely happy and mature for their age, polite, well mannered, and not at all what I think of as "spoiled." Like their parents, they often had what I would describe as a high degree of self-confidence, but not in an obnoxious way, and little or no sense of entitlement. They seemed more like the kids I grew up with forty years ago, and less like most kids I know today.

I was having trouble putting a name to this old-school parenting style, until I sat down with Julia and Gerald Thomson and they told me stories of the parents to whom they provide financial counseling through their church. "We call it the 'oxygen mask approach' to raising children," Gerald said.

I must have looked a little bewildered, or at least more so than usual. "You know," Julia said, "like in an airplane when they tell you to put your own oxygen mask on first before helping your children? At first it seems cruel or selfish, but when you think about it, ultimately it's the best thing you can do for your kids and your family. That's how we counsel the parents we work with to think when it comes to providing for themselves and their families, particularly when it comes to things like parents shorting their own retirement savings and financial security later in life in order to pay for their kid's college. Take care of your own financial needs first . . . the whole family . . . rather than always rushing to satisfy each child, because in the long run everyone will be better off because of it."

The kids of the cheapskate next door are expected to eat what's on the table, work hard for their allowance (if they receive one at all), get jobs outside the home as soon as they're old enough, and save up their own money to buy what they want, rather than go begging to Mom and Dad.

A majority of the cheapskate parents surveyed said that they would provide some financial assistance for their kid's college education, but they expected the child to shoulder much of that financial burden themselves. This was true even in cases where the parents were amassing retirement and other personal savings that could conceivably allow them to fund a greater portion of their children's education.

Call it old-school, call it tough love, call it the oxygen mask approach to parenting, but the cheapskates next door have a slightly different approach to bringing up baby. The cheapskates next door are determined to raise fiscally fit kids.

The Family Plan à la Cheapskate

In my first book, I wrote very little about children and parenting, trying instead to offer financial and lifestyle advice that I felt would benefit any American adult—single or married, young or old, big family or small.

I did, however, write the following: "It's also important to understand fully the potential financial impact of major decisions we make in our lives, even those decisions we make more from our hearts than from the financial lobes of our brains, things like having children . . ." And then I went on to mention that at that time (2006), according to Bankrate.com, it cost about $200,000 to raise a child from birth to age eighteen in the United States, not including the cost of private schools or college. In the same vein (and paragraph) I also mentioned that, according to the website aspca.org, it costs about $780 yearly to care for a midsize dog, which would total $14,040 for eighteen years. (NOTE: Those are eighteen human years, not dog years.)

I had more responses from readers regarding that paragraph than any other in the book, and not because they felt I was trying to equate children to midsize dogs (as I clearly wasn't). Rather, cheapskate parents from across the country wrote to say that the

$200,000-per-child cost estimate was "ridiculous," "absurd," "crazy," "some government research nonsense," and, plainly put, "bulls--t." In fact, a good many cheapskate parents assured me that the $780-per-year cost of raising a dog was, if anything, *high* compared to what they were actually spending to raise their kids, midsize or even larger.

Well, maybe they were exaggerating . . . or maybe not. Cheapskate Vickie Smith told me, "I figured it out to be closer to the cost to sponsor a child in a foreign country, so approximately $25 per month per child. In our case it's definitely cheaper by the dozen!" Smith is the mother of ten, and her family lives frugally but comfortably in Idaho on her husband's modest salary as a butcher.

In fairness, that $200,000 figure includes pro rata expenses for a child's housing (35 percent of the $200,000), transportation (14 percent), and health care (11 percent), in addition to the more directly allocable costs per child that Vickie is speaking about, including things like food, clothing, and entertainment. Even so, as we'll see throughout this book, the cheapskate next door knows the secrets for spending less on just about everything—from houses and insurance to groceries and recreation—so their child-rearing costs definitely drop proportionately.

Two-Income Families: A Necessity or a Choice?

Of that big old $200,000 pie chart, nearly $25,000 of it is spent on child care and education costs (again, not including the cost of private schools or college).

This touches on another very significant lifestyle difference between the cheapskate next door and the general U.S. population. Of those cheapskate families polled, only about 40 percent of those with children under the age of eighteen had both parents employed outside the home. This compares to more than 60 percent of such families nationwide, according to the Bureau of Labor Statistics. The frequency of single-income families among the cheapskates polled is roughly equivalent to the national rate of single-income families in the late 1970s. Once again, déjà vu from the America I grew up in.

It's fascinating to look at statistics (not to mention high school yearbooks) comparing lifestyles and finances today to those of the 1970s. In the early '70s, most American families still lived on a single income, whereas today, two breadwinners are the norm. A typical single-income family in the early '70s earned about $32,000 in today's inflation-adjusted dollars, compared to the average of $73,000 for a two-income family in the early 2000s. Even though the cost of clothing, food, appliances/electronics, and automobiles has actually *decreased* (again, in inflation-adjusted dollars) since the 1970s, the two-income family today is saving less than the single-income family managed to save in the '70s, and spending about 15 percent of its annual income to service revolving debt (as compared to less than 2 percent in the 1970s).

So, where is all that extra money in today's two-income families going? Well, we spend far more on housing than in the 1970s, that's for sure. But, as we'll in see Chapter 10, that's in large part because *we want more house* than we were satisfied with in the 1970s. We want about 40 percent more square feet in our homes than in the '70s (even though the average family size has decreased), and we want granite countertops, not Formica, and hot tubs as well as bathtubs.

The fact is, most of the extra money generated in many two-income families (at least in those with children) goes toward, well, generating that second income. When both parents work, we need to pay for child care, we usually need two cars, we usually pay higher taxes (because we earn more), and we usually eat more meals out, spend more on work clothing, and "treat" ourselves more often—because, you know, we're both working so hard and we deserve it.

"*Enough already!*" many cheapskate parents say. Let's skip the Money Step, as I called it in my first book, and have one parent stay home to raise our children, at least until they're in school and old enough to look after themselves. Sure, it means we'll have less stuff and a lower (gross) household income, but for the cheapskates next door the benefits of a one-income family often outweigh the costs.

Danny Kofke, a schoolteacher with a salary of $40,000 a year, and his wife have two young daughters. He told me: "We explained to our oldest daughter why she does not have as many materialistic things as her friends. She is starting to get to that age where she notices what others have. We've asked her if she would rather have more stuff and go to day care or have Mommy be at home with her, and she always says she would like to have Mommy at home instead."

None of this is to say that there's a bias against working moms among cheapskates. It's all about having the financial freedom—by virtue of leading a cheapskate lifestyle—to do whatever you want. Cheapskate Amy Williams has always chosen to be a working mom, even though she and her husband and two daughters could have lived comfortably on a single income. She enjoys her career as an interior designer, so that's what she chooses to do. When Amy's husband recently lost his job, the wisdom and virtue of the cheapskate lifestyle the Williamses have always led became apparent: With modest expenses and a healthy nest egg, the Williamses' life hasn't changed in the least since they involuntarily became a single-income family.

A Decision Not to Be Made Lightly

So, according to the cheapskates next door, it's definitely possible to raise happy, healthy children on an à la cheapskate plan, even on a single income. But the cheapskates next door don't make the decision to become parents lightly, even if they know how to raise quality kids on the cheap. Here are some comments on parenting that were echoed time and again by the cheapskates next door:

- "Don't rush into it! Wait at least a few years into your marriage before you even think about having kids. That way you'll be better able to afford them, and you'll know that your marriage is solid first." (Joe Johns, father of two)
- "We love all three of our kids, but think long and hard before you go for numero three. It means a minivan instead of a sedan, extra hotel rooms on vacation, probably an extra bedroom . . ." (Rachael Boxer, mother of three)
- "Get on a family budget before the baby comes. Work hard to manage your own wants and needs first. Work hard at staying married—a stable home makes a big difference, regardless of your wealth." (Bill Fox, father of four)
- "Make a 'business plan' just like you were starting a new business, because you are. You will be in the business of building children from scratch. There will be costs before they even come out of the oven, so get prepared." (Wayne Petitto, father of two)
- "It's OK for people to choose to not have children, or, if they want children, to get one that is already on the ground that no one wants. There needs to be serious social reinforcement that choosing *not* to have children is as legitimate as choosing to have children. You can lead a very happy, totally ful-

filling life without kids." (Bruce Ostyn and Daniel Newman, no children)

- "Go to the library and start reading *Parenting* magazine now. I wish I had! I think it would have opened my eyes more to the reality of parenting vs. the slick advertising fliers showing all the slick baby gear!" (Julie Hall, mother of two)

Just Say No (To Your Kids)

"Gratification is a dish best prepared in a Crock-Pot: nice and slow." I've heard a lot of cheapskate slogans that would make great bumper stickers for my Cheap Pride Movement, but that one from Miser Adviser Lucy Feller is the undisputed winner, combining the two major pillars of cheapskate life: delayed gratification and Crock-Pot cooking.

Lucy was speaking specifically about teaching children the importance of being patient, particularly when it comes to wanting things like the latest designer fashions or newest techno-gadget. Not only does she have three kids of her own, but she's been an elementary school teacher ever since her own children started attending school, so Lucy's had plenty of discussions about the virtues of delayed gratification.

The oxygen mask approach to raising children is, in large part, an exercise in saying "no" to your kids. *No*, we can't afford it. *No*, you can't have it. *No*, you don't need it. *No*, you'll just have to wait. And once again, for the cheapskate next door it's not primarily about the money; it's truly about the principle of the thing.

"You won't ruin your children's lives by not giving them cell phones, video games, cars, and unlimited TV, if you replace it with healthy family activities and love," John "Doc" Dochnahl told me. "They will thank you as adults." John has a son and daughter, both

CHEAP SHOT
TRUST FUND IN A BOX

Cheapskate Lenore Lenny and her husband aren't rich, but they're trying an interesting little experiment in creating trust funds of sorts for their two young sons. Every Christmas since their twins were born, the Lennys have bought four small, identical gift items, each costing $5 or less: things that are easily stored, like Christmas tree ornaments, books, DVDs, or small toys. On Christmas morning, the boys each open one of the matching presents. But unbeknownst to the twins, the two other identical gifts are deposited by their parents, unopened (i.e., in the "original packaging"), in a box labeled for each son. These are the twins' secret "Trust Funds in a Box," to be given to them on their twenty-first Christmas. No, the Lennys don't have fantasies about the memorabilia tucked away in the boxes appreciating in value and funding the twins' early retirement. But for the $105 they'll spend on the contents of each box, it is, as Lenore says, "more fun and probably better odds than $105 in lottery tickets." Future eBay hopes aside, the boys will have a time capsule of memories from their youth, and "some things to hopefully share with our grandchildren," Lenore adds. While investing in "collectibles" isn't usually wise, I'd pay $105 to see the expression on those kids' faces on their twenty-first Christmas.

Savings: Maybe a total loss, but always remember Beanie Babies.

now in their early twenties, who confirm the wisdom of their parents' child-rearing ways.

Another cheapskate put it this way: "The motivation is noble and heartfelt. Parents want to give their children what they want. But too often, in attempting to give our kids everything they want, whenever they want it, we're really doing three things: We're teaching them that, in life, you always get everything you want, as soon as you want it. Second, the child doesn't see or understand the behind-the-scenes consequences—that Mom and Dad are probably going into debt to give them everything they want. And, three, we're teaching kids that there's a relationship between giving 'stuff' . . . spending money . . . and showing 'love.' I think that last one's the most dangerous lesson we're teaching kids by spoiling them, even though we usually mean well by our actions."

And apparently "just saying no" pays off. In response to the question "Would you say your children are 'spoiled' compared to other children you know?," nearly 95 percent of cheapskate parents responded "No." While this is admittedly a subjective assessment, it's telling at least with regard to the parents' ambitions.

For the cheapskate next door, the oxygen mask approach to raising children has a very real impact on the bottom line of the family budget: Market research has shown that children directly and indirectly influence more than $700 billion in household spending every year. No wonder advertisements for everything from automobiles to vacation destinations, from restaurants to snack foods, frequently target kids. Advertisers know that while kids won't be buying most of those products and services themselves, they typically have a lot of clout with old Mom and Dad.

"That's one of the primary reasons we don't own a television," Wayne Curry told me. "We don't want our kids to be seduced by all that advertising . . . The advertisers aren't just trying to get in-

CHEAP SHOT
TOY LIBRARIES: AN IDEA
WHOSE TIME HAS COME

In Europe, Australia, and other places around the world, "toy libraries" are popular public institutions in towns and cities, small and large. A cheapskate who recently moved to the United States from Great Britain was shocked when she was house hunting here and asked the real estate agent about the toy libraries nearest to the neighborhoods she was considering. "The agent looked at me with a complete blank stare. At first I thought she didn't know where the nearest toy library was located. But then she told me she didn't even know what a toy library *was*!" Each year Americans spend about $22 billion on children's toys, the vast majority of which end up in the landfill in relatively short order. Thankfully, toy libraries are finally starting to spring up in the United States, where children can play with quality toys and/or borrow them to play with at home. Toy libraries are often operated in conjunction with existing book libraries, and sometimes they are established as independent organizations. Contact the USA Toy Library Association (USATLA.org) for a directory and more information, or get involved in your local public library and encourage them to add a line of donated toys.

Savings: Save just 25 percent of the $365 spent annually on toys for the average American child, and you'll be ahead by more than $90 per year, per child.

side the kid's piggy banks, they're trying to recruit our kids against us, so that they'll try to tell us what we need to buy."

Of the cheapskates polled, nearly 5 percent said they don't own and/or watch television, which is two to three times greater than the national average. And more than half said they watch less than one hundred hours of TV per month, with the national average being roughly one hundred and forty hours per month. So, if you're an advertiser trying to reach the cheapskate family market, you might want to cut back on your TV advertising budget.

Teach Your Children Well

"Jeff, I just have to tell you the funniest little story about my grandkids." Dave was a man probably in his mid-seventies who sat nodding enthusiastically throughout a book talk I gave at a public library during the Midwest leg of the Tour de Cheapskate. I could tell from the Santa-like sparkle in his eye that my words were resonating with him, as they often do with older folks who long ago came to understand that there's a lot more to life than money and stuff.

"You'll never guess what my grandkids want to do whenever we get together. All they want to do is play with Grandpa Dave's money! They never see money. Their parents charge everything. They think Grandpa Dave is the only person alive who actually has real money! Isn't that a sign of the crazy times we're living in?"

According to Nathan Dungan, author of the book *Prodigal Sons and Material Girls: How Not to Be Your Child's ATM* (Wiley, 2003) and founder of the organization Share, Save, Spend, fewer than 20 percent of American parents make any effort to teach their children about money. I heard Dungan speak a few years ago, and afterward I suggested to him that in fact 100 percent of American parents teach their kids about money—by virtue of the example they set every day. As a friend of mine put it, "Show me a spoiled kid, and I'll show you some spoiled parents. If kids get everything they want as soon as they want it, I'll bet they learned it by seeing how their parents live."

Because the cheapskates next door usually have their own financial house in order, they provide solid role models for their children. Day in and day out, cheapskate kids see their parents managing their money wisely, avoiding debt, and learning to delay discretionary purchases until they can truly afford them. Nearly 90 percent of the adult cheapskates polled said that they learned about money management, at least in part, by seeing the example set by their own frugal parents, and they're now passing down the same lessons to their children. Just like kids often pick up their parents' bad habits, they pick up their parents' good habits as well.

Hard-Earned (and -Learned) Allowance Plans

But as important as setting an example is, most cheapskates say that they also discuss money with their children starting at a very young age. Roughly eight out of ten of the cheapskate parents polled say that they make some formal effort to educate their kids about personal finances, nearly the mirror image of the national statistics mentioned by Nathan Dungan.

In most cases, a part of that education involves paying children an allowance or other money in exchange for performing household chores. About three-quarters of the cheapskate parents polled said that they provide some type of allowance/payment to their kids, often a weekly amount roughly equal to one-half to the equivalent of the child's age (e.g., a ten-year-old might receive $5–$10 per week). That's apparently on par with the national average for children's allowances, according to a survey by *Money* magazine.

It's worth noting that the 25 percent or so of cheapskate parents who don't provide allowances to their children often feel strongly about the issue. "You should not have to pay your children to hold up their end of the bargain—being part of the family and doing their share of the chores," Amy Williams told me. She and other non-allowance proponents also felt that an allowance discourages children from finding odd jobs and other work outside the home, which, the parents feel, can be a valuable learning experience for children starting at a relatively young age.

In cheapskate homes where kids do get an allowance, it's almost always tied to performing specific chores. In the vast majority of cases, the parents also set conditions on the child's "management" of the allowance, often structured around the three principles of *save, share, spend*. Children are expected to *save* a certain amount (often 20 percent) for long-term goals, *share* some amount (often 10 percent) with charities or others, and they're free to *spend* the remainder—unless, of course, they inherited their parents' Spending Anxiety Disorder, in which case their savings and sharing accounts will likely be the beneficiaries.

According to the cheapskate next door, it's never too early to start teaching your kids about money and the three principles of save, share, and spend. Cheapskate Stacie Barnett set up what she calls a "Candy Land–esque" chart on the fridge for her son when he was only seven years old. "Every time he did a chore, he'd move a space. The board was divided into three levels. When he hit Level One, I'd donate $1 to a charity of his choice. When he hit Level Two, $2 would go into his savings. At Level Three, he'd get $3 to spend. He could go as quickly or as slowly through the board as he wanted."

More Money Lessons for Raising Fiscally Fit Kids

In addition to the allowance system, the cheapskate next door involves the kids in other aspects of the family's finances as well.

Miser Adviser Pam Hanlon helped to teach her son about money and smart shopping—and got herself a much-needed helping hand in the grocery store—by taking him with her and letting him keep what he saved them with coupons. A number of other cheapskate families told me that they routinely involve their kids in grocery shopping, menu planning, and meal preparation as a way of not just teaching them about money, shopping, and cooking, but as a way of encouraging them to expand their tastes in foods and try new things.

Many cheapskate families say they turn over much or all of an annual "clothing allowance" directly to their kids (often in biannual or quarterly allotments) and entrust them to shop for their own clothing—and budget accordingly. If the child wants to buy something more expensive than their clothing budget allows, then they pay the balance from their own savings.

"It makes them a lot more interested in shopping at thrift stores when they can see how much further their money goes there—designer fashions and brand names aren't nearly as appealing," said cheapskate Emma Schmitz, mother of thirteen-year-old twins.

Another common practice among cheapskate families is to allow their children to sell the clothes they've outgrown at yard sales or resale shops and add the proceeds to their clothing fund. It's sort of the kid's own sinking fund for clothing.

And finally, one of the most touching stories I've heard of creative techniques for teaching money management to the next generation came from Amy and David Charlton of Bowling Green,

Ohio. For the past eight years, the Charltons have planted a two-acre vegetable garden in partnership with their grandchildren, ages eight to sixteen. Working together, they've sold the produce at a roadside stand, with all proceeds going into a special college fund the Charltons have set up for the grandchildren.

From planting to weeding to closing the sales with customers, the Charltons' grandchildren aren't just learning about the value of work and money, they're also spending precious time with their grandparents and building a not-insignificant college savings fund for themselves. Amy and David pay for all the seeds, fertilizers, and other costs, and they admit that to keep the kids motivated they sometime all agree to dip into the fund for something fun like tickets to an amusement park or the zoo. "It's allowed us to do something with our grandkids and give them something for college that we otherwise wouldn't have been able to give them," Amy told me.

By the way, one of the kids' zucchinis took the blue ribbon at the Wood County Fair the other year, and if you know the size of the zucchinis they grow in Ohio, that's no small accomplishment.

College: Time to Drink the Red Kool-Aid?

"The problem is, a college education just costs so much more than it used to." If I had a quarter for every time I've heard that over the last few years, I'd stop embarrassing my poooor wife by checking the coin return on every pay phone I pass. Well, maybe I would.

Whenever I speak at colleges, universities, and other public venues, it seems like the topic of student loans and the rising costs of a college education always comes up. Here are the facts: While costs at U.S. colleges and universities have indeed increased faster than the rate of inflation over the past few decades, they haven't skyrocketed as much as you might think.

According to the website FinAid.org, between 1958 and 2005 the "college inflation rate" averaged 6.89 percent while the "general inflation rate" averaged 4.15 percent. So the cost of college has increased at a rate of 1.66 times the rate of inflation. It's also worth noting that tuitions have tended to increase more slowly, only slightly faster than the rate of inflation, with the biggest percentage increases coming from room and board, textbooks, and other nontuition fees.

What's changed far more dramatically than the cost of a college education over the same time period is what we expect that college education to look like. Things like the prestige of the institution we want to attend, how and where we'll live while going to college, whether or not we're willing to work part-time or in the summers while going to school, how long we'll take to get our degree, and how we'll spend our free time (including spring breaks!) during our years in school. The days of living at home with your parents and attending a local college, busing tables to earn extra cash on spring break, and living off ramen noodles for four years are as long gone for most students today as fraternity hazing rituals and Pac-Man.

College is the point at which millions of Americans submerge for the first time under the waterline of personal debt, some never to get their heads fully above that red waterline again, ever. Roughly two-thirds of all students who graduated in 2008 with a four-year degree had some student loans, with the average being almost $23,000. This is the point where the cheapskate and the typical American part ways.

The cheapskates next door certainly value higher education. Of those polled, almost 60 percent had at least a four-year college degree, which is more than twice the national average. A similar percentage of cheapskate parents expect that their kids will also go to college, although only about 10 percent of those parents plan to pay the whole tab for their children's education. Another roughly 10 percent said they plan on offering no financial assistance whatsoever to their college-bound kids. The remaining 80 percent said they plan on offering partial assistance, ranging from providing free room and board if the child attends a local institution, to matching every dollar the child earns toward his own education either through work or scholarships.

So the cheapskate next door feels strongly about the value of getting a college degree. As cheapskate Brandan DuChateau was told by her mother, "an education is the one gift I can give you that no one can ever take away." But they also feel equally as strong about something else. "Don't go in debt for it!" screams Vickie Smith, talking about the importance of paying for your college degree as you go.

How to Graduate *Summa Cum Debt-Free*

"It's simple. In fact it's so simple that if you can't do it (go to college without going into debt), they shouldn't let you into college in the first place, because you're not smart enough." Well, that's the opinion of Brad Thorton, who proudly graduated three years ago—debt free—and without any financial assistance other than some modest book scholarships awarded because of his academic performance.

"It's like anything else," Brad told me. "You need to work and save and work and save in advance. Then you need to look at how much you have available to spend, and come up with a plan to fit that amount. Most people do just the opposite—decide what they want to do, *then* start to think about how they're going to pay for it. That's when they decide it's impossible, unless they borrow money."

In Brad's case, part-time jobs during high school and summer vacation earned him more than enough to attend a local community college for two years, where he took the basic required courses for a fraction of what they would have cost at a four-year institution. He then transferred to a local branch of a state college (which accepted the course credits from the community college), where he completed the remaining course work he needed in just over eighteen months. He continued to work part-time jobs as much as he could while going to school, and—most important—he lived at home, with his parents, the whole time.

"Yeah, sometimes I wished I'd gone away to school or lived on campus, but I love my parents and siblings, so living at home was cool. I have to laugh, though, because so many people I met who lived on campus took out these massive student loans, and so when they graduated, they were so broke that *then* they moved back home with Mom and Dad! Pretty ironic, isn't it?" "Ironic" seems hardly the word; maybe "stupid" is more accurate.

Brad's story includes several key strategies mentioned by many cheapskates in discussing how to graduate *summa cum debt-free*. Consider these and other nontraditional approaches to getting a college education, instead of just resigning yourself to drinking the red Kool-Aid and taking out student loans:

- **Live at home (or even with willing relatives!) and attend a nearby college.** Room and board add about $7,000 or more per academic year to the cost of college. Interesting, isn't it, that eliminating that one expense would more than allow most students to avoid borrowing a single dime in student loans?
- **Attend a community college for the first two years.** According to an article in *U.S. News & World Report*, in 2007 the average *annual* net tuition cost paid by community college students was only $320 for a full course load; that's less than two

weeks' pay at a minimum-wage job! Even after factoring in the cost of books (See Cheap Shot), supplies, and transportation, the article estimated that by living and eating at home, it would cost only about $2,500 per year to attend a community college for the first two years, as Brad did, before transferring those credits to a four-year institution. According to the same article, attending an in-state public university and living on campus would cost you about $15,500 per year—vs. $2,500 for the same credits at a community college; think about that before you decide to go into debt for a college degree.

- **Graduate in less than four years.** Although it might interfere with a student's ability to work part-time while going to school or in the summers, a number of cheapskates talked about what one called the "powering through school" approach. That means taking maximum course loads and attending school during summer sessions, when tuitions and fees are sometimes lower and courses tend to be easier (in part because of the shortened session) so that you can handle a heavier load. The strategy is to get out into your career field as quickly as possible—even if it means taking out student loans—since your earning potential at that point will be much greater than flipping burgers at the student union. Being smart about class scheduling and not continually changing majors/institutions can save you significant expense by allowing you to earn your degree as quickly as possible.

- **Graduate from the most prestigious school of all—"Ididitallbymyself University."** Over the years there have been many and conflicting reports about how much—if at all—employers value degrees from certain "prestigious" colleges and universities more than those from public and other less-respected private institutions. Speaking as a former employer of a good many college graduates—and reinforced by many conversations I've had with others who manage workforces of their own—I can tell you this: I was infinitely more impressed by an individual who worked his or her way through college and maintained good grades, than by the name of the institution from which they graduated. Give me a graduate from a state school who did it all by himself any day, over an Ivy Leaguer who got a free ride from Mom and Dad or who is up to his mortarboard in student-loan debt.

- **Other Cheapskate options:**
- Receiving college credit toward your degree by taking College Level Examination Program (CLEP) tests instead of some college classes (CollegeBoard.com/student/testing/clep/about).
- Exploring military service (Military.com/education-home) and other public service programs and jobs (AmeriCorps.gov) that entitle you to attend college for free or at a significant savings.
- Looking into work-study programs (ED.gov/programs/fws/) and paid internships (CampusInternships.com) that can earn you extra money and career-related experience.
- Letting your employer pay for your degree, particularly for an advanced degree. More than 90 percent of those cheapskates polled who have advanced degrees earned them with at least partial financial support from their place of employment.
- And, of course, pursuing college scholarships and grants (CollegeScholarships.org).
- If, in the end, a cheapskate does decide to take out a student loan, she borrows the absolute minimum and pays it off as quickly as possible, before she even thinks about assuming additional debt (e.g., car loan, credit cards, mortgage, etc.). The National Student Loan Program (NSLP.org) is an excellent resource regarding student loan options.

CHEAP SHOT
TEXTBOOK TRAVAILS

According to the *Chronicle of Higher Education*, the average four-year-college student now spends almost $1,000 per academic year on textbooks. Think of the ramen noodles that would buy! Fortunately, the Internet has made the buying and selling of used textbooks much easier than it was back in my college days, when you'd spend days staking out the used-books aisle at the campus bookstore, waiting for someone to come in and sell a used copy of *Gray's Anatomy* (the textbook that is, not the TV show). Save up to 80 percent on textbooks by buying them used on websites like BetterWorldBooks.com, Textbooks.com, CampusBooks.com, and BookFinder.com. You can also *rent* textbooks at Skoobit.com. Always find out the exact International Standard Book Number (ISBN) of the textbook you're looking for, and go online at ISBN.nu to compare prices from various retailers. Keep your receipts, just in case you bought the wrong book or end up dropping the class. Shop for used books early for the best selection, and sell any unwanted textbooks immediately after the class ends for the best trade-in prices.

Savings: Buying used textbooks can easily save you 50 percent, or **$500** off the $1,000 average annual figure mentioned above.

CHAPTER 5

Thrift:
The Greenest Shade of Green

When at home, urinate on your lemon tree.
—A Miser Adviser from Australia, with a tip for conserving water (folks say she makes the best lemonade Down Under)

I've been a tree-hugging environmentalist since long before it was cool, from way back in my early teens, when my long hair and eunuch-like sexual aura regularly got me mistaken for Tiny Tim, of *Rowan & Martin's Laugh-In* fame.

For me, the connection between spending and consuming less in order to help save the planet has always been obvious. Although just the other day a friend of mine questioned my credentials as both an environmentalist and a cheapskate when he discovered that I use disposable razors. "What do you expect?" I said, indignantly. "I hardly ever find the other kind in my neighbor's trash."

That's right. Go ahead. Just try me. I'm cheap and I'm green, through and through. In fact, I would argue that you can't be the former without also being the latter, even if unintentionally.

I think it's great that more and more Americans are finally embracing the environmental movement. The planet needs all the help she can get, provided that it's not too late already. But I think there's a bit of hypocrisy at play. You see, if you're an average American, you can't honestly embrace the green movement without also accepting that it means that you need to consume—and therefore probably spend—a lot less in your own life.

CHEAP SHOT
GREEN CLEAN WITH COMMON HOUSEHOLD PRODUCTS

The production and disposal of many household cleaning products is an environmental nightmare, and eco-friendly cleaning products are often much more expensive than their toxic competitors. No worries. The following cleaning techniques, which use common household products, are even lighter on the environment than most store-bought "green cleaners," not to mention lighter on your wallet:

- Polish furniture with a cloth dipped in cool black tea, and clean wood floors with a solution of one part lemon juice to two parts vegetable oil.
- Toothpaste will make your silver shine; use ketchup to polish copper.
- A simple solution of baking soda and water (one part baking soda to five parts water) will clean appliances, countertops, and even your oven.
- Olive oil dissolves tar, a pencil eraser removes heel marks, and a wet pumice stone scrubs away rust and other stains on porcelain.

Savings: Use these eco-gentle household products instead of the toxic alternatives or pricey green cleaning products and save at least $50–$100 a year.

Americans are only 5 percent of the world's population, but we consume roughly 30 percent of the world's resources. According to the World Wildlife Fund, if everyone on the planet consumed at the levels that we do here in the United States, it would take three planet Earths to provide the resources necessary to sustain that level of consumption. So, unless the universe runs a buy-one-get-one-free deal on new planets, we'll be screwed if everyone starts following America's lead when it comes to ripping through our natural resources.

Can the cheapskate next door save the planet? Maybe so.

Living Green vs. Spending Green

The cheapskates next door may not always talk the talk when it comes to the environmental movement, but boy do they ever walk the walk. Nearly as many cheapskates reported "little" or "no" interest in environmental issues as expressed a "strong" interest and involvement in such issues. Yet their near-unanimous commitment to living by the old environmentalist mantra—*reduce, reuse, recycle*—is truly a case of actions speaking louder than words.

Even among those cheapskates who are ardent environmentalists, I found that they share my sense of skepticism (bordering on cynicism) when it comes to buying specialized "green products." Only about 10 percent of those polled said that buying environmentally friendly products is a high priority when they shop. Daniel Newman told me, "Cheap equals green. I'd go a step further and say that cheap is the *only* green. It's not about consuming green products. It's about consuming less."

Many of my fellow cheapskates and I find it rather amusing that the thing that seems to be fueling the newfound popularity of the environmental movement here in the United States is, arguably, the very same thing that the movement should be seeking to change. I speak, of course, of rampant consumerism. The type that long ago stopped being about getting what we need or what we really even want, and is now simply about the mindless act of *getting.* As Danny Kaye said in *The Court Jester,* "Get it? Got it? Good!"

It seems as if the green movement in the United States really took off only after businesses got with the program and came out

---

CHEAP SHOT
LEECHES! I HATE LEECHES!

In case you don't recognize it, that's a Humphrey Bogart line from one of my all-time favorite movies, *The African Queen.* It's also been my rallying cry around the house (delivered in my best Bogey impersonation) ever since I learned that many household appliances use electricity even when they're turned off. Electrical leeches (aka "vampires") include your TV, DVD player, stereo, cell phone charger, computer, and microwave oven—in general, any electrical appliance that has a standby mode or one of those square transformer-type plugs. According to experts, these power suckers add 5 to 10 percent, or even more, to the typical electric bill. Unplug electrical leeches when they're not in use, or for greater convenience attach multiple appliances to a single power strip (like my favorite, the Gem Sound SP-8500) that can easily be flipped on and off.

Savings: A 10 percent savings on the average U.S. household electric bill would be more than $120 a year.

with supercool and super-expensive "green products." From hybrid automobiles to high-fiber cereals, from eco-chic running shoes to eco-friendly beers and wines, a *cause de stuff* was born.

This revelation kicked me in the butt like a giant carbon footprint one day when I saw a segment on a morning news show about "eco-friendly fashions." The runway model was sporting a skimpy (and, yes, very sexy) dress. I was shocked to hear the price—nearly $900—but then it started to make sense. The dress, they said, was made out of hemp.

Eyeing the runway model and mentally backing out what I estimated to be her 103.69 pounds of bulimic body weight, I figured you'd be left with the better part of a pound of hemp. Thinking back to that infamous Bachman-Turner Overdrive concert I attended at the Toledo Sports Arena in 1974, and adjusting for inflation, that seemed reasonable enough. If anything, at that price it must not be very good s--t. And if she smoked her own dress, what would the poor girl wear?

It's Easy Being Green, When You're Cheap

Cheapskates aren't the only Americans who are prone to be *accidentally green*, helping the environment perhaps more out of concern for their own pocketbooks than for Mother Earth herself. A 2009 study commissioned by Element Hotels, an eco-friendly lodging chain, found that 41 percent of the people they surveyed said that their vigilance about conserving resources (e.g., turning off lights and appliances, water conservation, etc.) was due primarily to economic considerations. Only 28 percent claimed environmental impact as their primary motivation.

It truly is easy being green, if you're cheap. Here are a couple of examples from some of my cheapskate friends:

- **"Not in the dishwasher! That's where we keep the ramen noodles for our camping trips!"** Daniel said as I headed across the *Architectural Digest*–gorgeous kitchen toward the dishwasher, carrying a stack of dirty plates. Trying to be a good houseguest, I was helping Daniel Newman and Bruce Ostyn with the dinner dishes during my stay with them. Daniel and Bruce, like a number of cheapskate families I visited, usually wash their dishes by hand. While both the economic and environmental impact of machine washing vs. hand washing can be debated, these guys have the system dialed—one dishpan for washing, one for rinsing—which definitely uses less energy and soap, and wastes no water, since both dishpans are promptly emptied directly onto their Arizona-thirsty plantings in the backyard. "Plus," Bruce adds, "washing the dinner dishes gives us a little time to talk and catch up with each other at the end of the day." One hastens to add that a dishwasher used exclusively for storing ramen noodles must last a heck of a lot longer.

- **"I know it looks like crap, but I can't see it, because I'm sleeping."** Carol McAnulty is proudly showing me the two-inch-thick pieces of robin's-egg-blue foam insulating board she cut herself to fit snugly on the inside of the windows in her ranch-style home on the shores of picturesque Platte Lake. She installs them only after dark—"It just takes a second," she says—and they've cut her winter heating bill by more than half. "Plus, this way I don't need to buy drapes or curtains!" she adds, rightfully reveling in her resourcefulness. Sealing doors, windows, and household cracks is always a good investment of time and money, and usually something you can easily do yourself. Beefing up insulation in walls, attics, crawl spaces, and elsewhere is also usually a sound investment, if you consider what you already have and the cost of upgrading. But when it comes to replacing windows solely to save energy, be careful. The high cost of window replacement can often make it a losing financial proposition. Do your homework before you do your home work: Request an energy audit (usually free) from your local utility company and visit EnergyStar.gov for bright ideas on saving energy.

- **"Since we are 'green bugs,' we designed our backyard to be drought tolerant,"** wrote David and Caroline Llewellyn of Euless, Texas, "which included doing away with all grass and making use of stone and rock along with native plants that require very little water. Our overall plan has eliminated the use of city water for our yard, and our water bill has been cut almost in half." The Llewellyns aren't the only cheapskates living next door who are cutting the grass, so to speak, by reducing the size of or entirely eliminating their traditional lawns. *Xeriscaping*—landscaping in such a way as to eliminate the need for supplemental irrigation (see Xeriscape.org)—and utilizing ground covers and other plant materials that don't require toxic fertilizers and pesticides, can save both time and money, not to mention Mother Earth. Popular low-maintenance ground covers include plants like ivy, creeping thyme, pachysandra, phlox, and everything from moss to yucca, depending on your climate. Lawn care services and supplies in the United States is a $12-billion-a-year industry. How much of that green is coming out of your pocket?

- **"As I like to say, I've been in hot water my whole life. My wife says I run hot and cold,"** Ed told me with a self-deprecating roll of his eyes. I guess if you've spent the past twenty-seven years installing and servicing hot-water heaters, as has Ed Boyle (real name, honest to God), you're entitled to a little tepid humor. According to Ed, about 15 percent of home heating costs are just for heating hot water, and that's no joke. He says you can reduce that cost by up to 50 percent— which means a hefty 7.5 percent decrease in your *total* house-

CHEAP SHOT
EVIAN IS *NAÏVE* SPELLED BACKWARD

Being a professional cheapskate, I'm frequently asked if I buy bottled water. "Heck no," I say in all truthfulness. "I don't even buy bottled wine." Prepare for shock and awe: 1.5 million barrels of oil are used every year to manufacture disposable plastic water bottles for the U.S. market. That's enough to fuel 100,000 cars for a year. The bottling process itself uses two gallons of water for every gallon of water it bottles. But regardless of whether or not the cheapskates next door are environmentalists, here's why they ain't buyin' it: Bottled water is 240 to 10,000 times more expensive than water from the tap, usually costing more than $10 a gallon . . . Think about *that* the next time you complain about gas prices. And bottled water is actually subjected to *less rigorous* testing and purity standards than tap water here in the United States. Use the calculator at newdream.org to calculate your savings based on actual consumption.

Savings: Variable, but according to an article in the *New York Times*, if you drink only bottled water you'll spend about $1,400 annually to get your recommended daily amount of H_2O, as opposed to 49 cents for a year's supply of just-as-healthy tap water.

hold heating bill—with a couple of simple steps, including: wash clothes in cold water only; turn down your hot-water heater to 110 degrees and/or turn it off overnight (you can also install an automatic timer to do the job); insulate your hot-water heater; install efficient showerheads. Those last two tips are inexpensive, do-it-yourself projects, so no need to call on Ed's services unless you're looking for a stand-up act for a special event. Ed says he specializes in "bath mitzvahs and wedding showers."

CHAPTER 6

Clean Your Plate . . . and Save $1,500 a Year

**The average American throws away almost a pound
of food per day. That's like throwing away an
Olsen twin every other month.**
—The Ultimate Cheapskate

I met Justin Thomas, an education specialist at the Naval Air Station in Lemoore, California, when I spoke at a financial seminar being held on the base for enlisted personnel. It was a real honor to speak to men and women who spend their days defending our nation and its freedoms.

Given modest military pay scales, I wasn't surprised to encounter a good many attendees at the seminar that day who shared with me wonderful dollar-stretching tips and stories of their own. Justin told me a story over lunch that I'll never forget.

Like most cheapskates, Justin despises wastefulness. In part, he says, it's because he's lived overseas extensively and recognizes that Americans tend to be more wasteful than people in many other countries of the world. For Justin, reducing waste is not just about saving money; it's truly the principle of the thing.

To his wife's chagrin, Justin is a proud "table poacher," occasionally helping himself to leftovers off the tables vacated by fellow restaurant patrons. "It's just a free appetizer," he explains, "something to nibble on before our own dinner arrives." Justin specifically tries to make it a point to do a little table poaching when dining out with his three young children, hoping to teach them a lesson about not wasting food and perhaps something even more important about humility.

So, one evening the Thomas family was dining out at a local pizza parlor. Justin's wife excused herself from the table to use the restroom after the family finished ordering their dinner. Justin noticed that a woman and child seated at the table next to them had been served an entire pizza, eaten only a couple of slices, and then left the restaurant.

Recognizing a teachable moment—and free pizza—when he sees it, Justin delivered his usual mini-sermon on waste to his three kids before stealthily sliding four pieces of the abandoned pizza onto the Thomases' table.

Despite his kids' embarrassment over their father's radical restaurant behavior, the rescued pizza was still hot and delicious, and the four of them wolfed it down. Justin's wife returned from the restroom just as they'd finished the free appetizers, none the wiser about what her husband and the kids had been up to.

Justin was feeling pretty smug. Until, that is, the woman and child who had been sitting next to them returned to their table and discovered that the better half of their pizza was missing. Apparently they had just run out for a moment to fetch something from their car.

As Justin says in a pitch-perfect imitation of Ricky Ricardo, "There was some splainin' to do that evening," both to the owner of the pillaged pizza and to Justin's mortified wife, who learned about the table poaching incident only as Justin publicly confessed to all involved. Once again, *c'est la cheapskate.*

Talkin' Trash

According to the U.S. Department of Agriculture (USDA), roughly 25 percent of all food purchased by Americans goes to waste. Sadly, when it comes to our food supply, we have crossed the line between the land of plenty and the land of squandering.

In a world in which more than a billion people go hungry every day, the cheapskates next door are doing their part to reduce food waste, reporting that they throw away an average of only about one-tenth of the amount discarded by the typical American household. I know; I sound like your mother trying to get you to clean your plate ("Children are starving to death in India!"), but Mom was right. Sure, wasting less here in the United States won't by itself solve world hunger, but what possible justification can there be for letting food go to waste?

"Lately I have come to consider that my extreme aversion to waste has something to do with my family history, and that I am a child of Holocaust survivors," Vera Meyer of Malden, Massachusetts, told me. Relying heavily on her trusty food dehydrator (see Cheap Shot), she says she wastes "not a morsel, ever," and I believe her.

Yet again, the cheapskate's decision to waste less is not only the right thing to do, but it can result in significant financial savings, particularly over time. With the average U.S. household spending more than $6,000 per year on food, the cheapskate next door is saving close to $1,500 by largely eliminating food waste through smarter food storage and portion control. Plug that annual savings into your compound interest calculator, and you'll see that it'll easily result in six-figure savings over your adult lifetime.

"We don't throw a lot of food away," writes Jean Chapman, "but every time I do, I picture throwing money into the garbage . . .

If you don't have time to use it before it goes bad, it's not a deal."
True, but what's the solution?

CHEAP SHOT
THE AFTERLIFE OF BREAD

My great-grandmother so preferred the crustiness of
the bread she grew up eating in Czechoslovakia that when
she moved to this country she'd let her store-bought
American-style bread go stale before she ate it. Indeed,
stale bread should be treasured, not trashed. Here's what
the cheapskates next door are making with their bread
when it gets a little stiff: bread crumbs, croutons, bread
soups, bread salads, bread puddings, and French toast
(stale bread was the original motivation behind this dish).
You can also try reviving stale bread by dipping it in
water and baking it in a 370-degree oven for twelve minutes or in a microwave for thirty seconds, but that would
just break my great-grandmother's heart.

Savings: Salvage a loaf or two of stale bread a
month—or buy some cheap "day old" bread at the
bakery—and you'll save some dough, like $50–$100
a year.

Take the Layover Pledge

Cheapskate Martha Miller told me that at their house they don't
have "leftovers," they have "layovers." That's because the Millers
have vowed to consume any remainders within twenty-four hours
after the meal.

"This simple idea has saved us so much money and really made
our lives easier," she says. "It cuts down on the number of meals

you have to prepare, and it also gives you a much better sense of portion control—how much you need to make in the first place."

In keeping with the Layover Pledge, in most cheapskate homes, dinner leftovers become the next day's lunch, or the next night's dinner. But at Beth Holovach's home, in Scott City, Kansas, "dinner leftovers become breakfast. Period." Nearly everyone agreed: If leftovers can't be used within a day or two, they go promptly into the freezer for future use.

Another favorite cheapskate strategy for managing leftovers is—you guessed it—*soup*. Carol Foote, of Queensbury, New York, calls it her "Clean out the Fridge Soup." What's the recipe? Whatever leftovers and other remnants you have on hand. Typically, individual leftover items (no matter how small the portion) are frozen in inexpensive plastic sandwich bags or containers and then kept together in the freezer in a larger sealed container or ziplock bag (aka "The Soup Sack") for additional freezer protection and convenience. Every couple of weeks, the Soup Sack is raided to throw together an unforgettable—and truly one of a kind—pot of Clean out the Fridge Soup.

But Is It Still Good?

As my pooooor wife says, "If you are what you eat, my husband should be reduced for quick sale." She's just kidding, for the most part. Here's the official scoop from the USDA on when it's still safe to buy and eat perishable items:

- A **"Sell By"** date tells the store how long to display the product for sale. You should buy the product before the date expires.
- A **"Best If Used By (or Before)"** date is recommended for best flavor or quality. It is not a purchase or safety date.

• A **"Use By"** date is the last date recommended for the use of the product while at peak quality. The date has been determined by the manufacturer of the product.

The USDA also says that because "Use By" dates usually refer to best quality and are not safety dates, "even if the date expires during home storage, a product should be safe, wholesome, and of good quality—if handled properly and kept at 40°F or below." See fsis.usda.gov for more details on food handling and storage.

CHEAP SHOT
ROOT CELLARS: THE NEW WINE CELLARS?

Home wine cellars are so old-economy. Why not be a trendsetter like cheapskate Ed Lutz and be the first family in your neighborhood with a good old-fashioned root cellar? They've been around for centuries, and they're making a comeback as an electricity-free way of storing fruits and vegetables using the natural ground temperature to good advantage. If constructed and maintained properly, they keep produce edible far longer than the fridge does, and are particularly practical for storing large quantities, including things that you plan to can later. Ed lives in rural Pennsylvania and made his "twenty-first-century root cellar" out of an old refrigerator that was beyond repair. Instead of pitching it, he buried it in the backyard using plans he found on ehow.com.

Savings: Variable, depending on use, but Ed says he saved at least the $50 he'd have paid to have his old fridge hauled away. That's one way of looking at it.

Keeping It Fresh

In addition to preserving food through dehydration (see Cheap Shot), canning and freezing are popular among the cheapskates next door. About a quarter of those polled said they can at least some of their own food, and slightly more than half own one or more stand-alone freezers. Even single cheapskates and those with smaller families, who were far less likely to own a stand-alone freezer, frequently discussed their practices for freezing foods promptly in the freezer compartment of their refrigerator rather than letting them go to waste.

Moisture-proof packing is a must to prevent freezer burn and preserve food quality while in the freezer. Aluminum foil and plastic containers will suffice, although a number of cheapskates, including Kate Easlick, recommend the "double plastic bag" method: putting individual smaller items in inexpensive plastic sandwich bags, and then putting a number of those smaller bags in larger (and more expensive!) ziplock freezer bags. That way the ziplock doesn't have direct contact with the food and you can reuse it for years.

Other cheapskate freezer tips include:

- Put plastic bottles three-quarters full of water in your freezer if it is nearly empty, to reduce temperature variations.
- Keep longer-term items in the coldest part of the freezer (the top shelf in upright models, and on top of the compressor step in chest-style freezers).
- Try to keep your freezer as full as possible to increase energy efficiency; in the event of a power outage, foods in a full freezer will stay frozen two to four days (if left unopened), while foods in a half-full freezer may thaw in only about twenty-four hours.

- Be careful about freezing most dairy products. Many, such as sour cream, yogurt, cream cheese, butter, and some softer cheeses, can be frozen but may change in consistency and taste. It's best to use such items in cooking if you've stored them in the freezer.
- When freezing vegetables, it's usually best to blanch them first (i.e., place them in boiling water for two minutes or so, then plunge them into ice water) before packing in airtight containers and placing in the freezer. Consult online resources (below) for freezing instructions regarding specific types of vegetables.

"For me, canning is first and foremost an enjoyable hobby," says cheapskate Dotty Neil, "but it's one that you'll enjoy again and again, every time you pop open a jar of homemade preserves, canned peaches, whatever." Home canning is apparently experiencing a resurgence due to the tightening economy and the increasing popularity of home gardens. Ball Brand Fresh Preserving Products reported that sales of its canning jars and supplies were up 30 percent in 2008.

Dotty's advice is to start out small, maybe try your hand at some easy-to-make "freezer jams," and pick up a good book on the subject at the local library, like *Ball Complete Book of Home Preserving* (Robert Rose, 2006). "Getting pickled" is also a good option for beginners, since it's possible to pickle many items—cucumbers, eggs, green tomatoes, garlic, beets, etc.—simply by cooking them on the stovetop and placing them in vinegar in the refrigerator, rather than sealing them in canning jars for long-term storage.

For more information on storing food in your freezer or refrigerator, by canning, or by other means, the cheapskates next door recommend:

- National Institute of Food and Agriculture (nifa.usda.gov)
- U.S. Food and Drug Administration (FoodSafety.gov)
- Health Goods (HealthGoods.com); see the Recommended Food Storage Chart
- *Emergency Food Storage & Survival Guide* (Three Rivers Press, 2002)
- *Putting Food By* (Plume, 1992)

CHEAP SHOT
DEHYDRATE FOODS FOR BIG SAVINGS

Okay, maybe a root cellar isn't for everybody, but an electric food dehydrator is, at least according to Vera Meyer. "The frugal device I treasure most is my food dehydrator, because I buy fresh stuff at reduced prices that needs to be dealt with quickly before it goes bad, and then I dry it, so that I can eat my dried apples, tomatoes, or even shrimp all year long," Vera says. By removing the water contained in foods, dehydrating concentrates the flavors and preserves the nutrients in a wide range of fruits, vegetables, meats, fish, herbs, nuts, grains, and even some dairy products. Once dehydrated, foods can last up to two years or even longer with airtight storage. Many can be eaten as-is or be rehydrated before using. Expect to pay about $100 for a good dehydrator that will last many years.

Savings: Variable, but Vera says her beloved dehydrator easily saves her **$200** a year or more by enabling her to buy items when they're least expensive and use them later.

CHAPTER 7

Come on and Take a FREE Ride

All things are cheap to the saving, dear to the wasteful.
—Benjamin Franklin

Talk about Tightwad Envy (TE): Half a year into my research for this book, I'd listened to more stories than I could keep track of in my growing stack of spiral notepads about cheapskates scoring free stuff—from dumpsters, junkyards, roadsides, giveaways, you name it. But now I wasn't just hearing about another free score. I was literally sitting in one.

I was sitting in a nicely upholstered, deliciously comfortable, overstuffed chair, interviewing Kate Easlick in the living room of her sunny little home, set in the Van Gogh–esque rolling fruit orchards of northern Michigan. "Yes, the chair and most of the rest of the furniture in here I either got for free or for just a few dollars at yard sales or thrift stores," she said.

Okay, if you're a cheapskate I'm sure you're not overly impressed. We all pride ourselves on such finds. But I hadn't traveled all the way to Benzonia, Michigan, to talk with Kate about her free chair. I was there to hear about her house. The house she got for free.

Kate, who raised two children on her own on just a part-time nurse's salary, put ads in the local paper and on community bulletin boards asking if anyone had a house they were going to tear down. Her proposal: to move an unwanted house—at her own expense— to the acreage she owned at the edge of town, saving the owners the demolition and disposal costs. Fortunately, Benzonia is a lake resort community, so it wasn't long before Kate found a quaint little summer cottage that was slated for demolition, and she nabbed herself a free home.

"It only cost $6,500 to move the cottage here, and we put about another $20,000 into building the foundation, basement, remodeling, and so on," she told me. Kate is deservedly proud of her sixteen-acre farmstead, a place locals sometime call "Whole Wheaty Hill," referring to her hippyish past and her ongoing commitment to leading a simple, environmentally responsible lifestyle. "There's no way I could have afforded a home like this if I hadn't done it this way, plus it's such a great story that it makes this place all the more special to me," she said.

As I got ready to leave Whole Wheaty Hill, I commented on a large, handsome-looking barn behind the house. Kate had a sly smile on her face, the same one she'd flashed when I first asked her about her house.

"Don't tell me," I said.

"No, it wasn't free," she responded, "but I only paid $250 for it and moved it here board by board myself."

And the little travel trailer that sits out by the road on her property? "Oh, that? It's not mine," she said. "It belongs to the state. It's an ozone-monitoring station, and I agreed to let them park it here if they paid me enough to cover all my property taxes."

As I drove off, I was feeling a little strange. I concluded that I was either going through male menopause and having a hot flash, or else my TE was definitely flaring up that day.

Free at Last, Free at Last . . . Thank the Internet, Free at Last

Despite my rather jaded opinion of computer technology in general, I'll admit that the Internet has its advantages, including making access to free stuff easier than ever. It's sort of like virtual dumpster diving.

The first tip from the cheapskate next door when it comes to using the Internet to find free stuff is to join local "reuse groups" in your area. Reuse groups are community-based networks of folks who have things they're looking to give away, and other people who are looking for specific items they'd prefer to get for free. Items to be given away and items wanted are posted by members on the Internet. It's not swapping, because one item isn't traded for another, and no money changes hands. It's all about keeping stuff out of the landfills and putting it in the hands of people who can use it. People of every economic and social background are encouraged to participate.

The largest network of reuse groups is affiliated with the Freecycle Network (see Cheap Shot), but a complete directory of local reuse groups is available on green.yahoo.com. Also check out ReUseItNetwork.org and the "Free" stuff listed in the For Sale category for each city featured on Craigslist.org.

Here are some other favorite places to score free stuff online, according to the cheapskates next door:

- **Free software** (OpenOffice.org): Free alternative to Microsoft Office. Bill Gates, watch your back, there's a cheapskate on your tail.
- **Free meals for the kids** (MyKidsEatFree.com): A nationwide directory of thousands of restaurants where kids can eat for free when accompanied by an adult.

- **Free audio books** (LibriVox.org): Volunteers record books found in the public domain (i.e., no longer covered by copyright), and you can download their recordings from this nonprofit website.

- **Free calling** (Skype.com): Use Skype software and worldwide computer-to-computer calling is free. Another cheap—but not free—favorite is the $40 magicJack device (magicJack.com) that plugs into the USB port on your computer and allows you to make unlimited local and domestic long-distance calls for $20 a year.

- **Free foreign languages** (bbc.co.uk/languages): Jumpstart your training in a wide range of foreign languages using these online audio and visual teaching tools, compliments of the British Broadcasting Corporation.

- **Free puppy love** (Petfinder.com): Search a nationwide index of pets available for adoption from humane societies and other animal shelters.

- **Free stuff on your birthday** (FrugalLiving.tv/free-stuff/birthday-freebies.html): An unscrupulous acquaintance of mine claims it's his birthday whenever he eats in a restaurant. Based on the number of free pieces of birthday cake he's finagled, the jerk is over 1,200 years old. Check out this website for an impressive list of legitimate freebies you're entitled to on your birthday.

- **Free wheels** (AutoDriveaway.com): Plan your travel around transporting someone else's car, and you'll avoid rental fees and other costs.

- **Free cocktails** (MyOpenBar.com): I stopped at a tavern once on the Tour de Cheapskate that had a sign above the bar reading FREE BEER TOMORROW. I was so excited that I changed my travel plans so I could go back the next day to partake. The sign said the same thing the next day, but the bartender got a good laugh out of it. MyOpenBar can help hook you up with free—or really cheap—drinks in various cities.

- **More free stuff!:** Other top sites for product samples and all things free include: TheFreeSite.com, StartSampling.com, freechannel.net, Freenology.com, and the granddaddy of free-stuff websites, Volition.com.

CHEAP SHOT
DON'T JUST RECYCLE—FREECYCLE

Looking for a secondhand bicycle or maybe a dining room set, but a little short on cash? What if you could get it for free? The Freecycle Network (Freecycle.org) is an international nonprofit organization dedicated to keeping good stuff out of landfills by connecting folks who have something they no longer need with someone else who can use it (and the other way around). Through almost 5,000 community-based Freecycle groups, members list things on the Freecycle website that they're looking to give away or hoping to receive. The catch: This is straight-up "gifting"—trading or charging for items is prohibited. Anyone can participate, regardless of economic status, as it's all about reuse, reduce, recycle.

Savings: The sky's the limit. I recently saved more than $250 on some lumber and other building supplies I got for free through the Freecycle Network.

The Scavenging Lifestyle

"When I was a kid, my father was always asking me what I wanted to be when I grew up. 'Do you want to be a ballerina, honey? Or maybe a doctor or a lawyer? What do you want to be?' " Anneli

Rufus, now nearly fifty, told me the story of how her father became increasingly frustrated by her lack of career interests as a child.

"Finally, one day, he said, in total sarcasm, 'What are you going to be . . . a *beachcomber*?' And I said 'Yes, that's what I want to be. I want to be a beachcomber.' " Her father laughed at the time, but Anneli was quite serious and she has become just that.

"We're full-time scavengers," she says, speaking of her life with her husband, Kristan Lawson. They're also the authors of *The Scavengers' Manifesto* (Tarcher, 2009), which they describe as "the new handbook for the scavenging movement." Anneli and Kristan broadly define scavenging as "any legal way to get stuff for less than full price," so it's everything from thrift-store shopping and using coupons to dumpster diving, foraging for wild foods, and, yes, beachcombing.

We immediately hit it off, since, like me, the couple's means of support consists of two components: the modest income common among writers like us and, much more important, the fact that we don't need to spend much money to live comfortably. "The way we live, our scavenging lifestyle, has definitely allowed us to pursue our passion for writing as a career," Kristan said. "Spending nothing is the equivalent of earning something."

It was love at first sight between Anneli and Kristan, who met when they were both attending the University of California in Berkeley. "The first time I saw him, I could tell that he was wearing clothes from the thrift store, even though at that time used clothing wasn't cool," Anneli told me. Kristan grew up poor, in a single-parent household in which thrift was a matter of course. Anneli was raised in a middle-class but frugal family. "We were the Jewish family who was always first in line at the store the day after Easter to buy the discounted Easter candy," she said with a chuckle.

The couple lives debt-free, except for the remainder owed on the mortgage for their home in the hills overlooking San Francisco Bay. Anneli and Kristan say they go for days—sometimes even weeks—without once opening their wallets. They rely on public transportation and shoe leather to get around town ("You'd be sur-

CHEAP SHOT
FREE MONEY?!

Be still, my Inner Miser. The National Association of Unclaimed Property Administrators (NAUPA) says that one out of eight people in the United States has unclaimed assets, with claims averaging about $1,000 each. I didn't believe this until I did a search of my own and turned up a small amount of funds my family was eligible to collect on behalf of a deceased relative. Unclaimed assets include everything from forgotten bank accounts and inheritances to utility-bill refunds, security deposits, and a wide range of other funds. Assets like these are commonly turned over to state treasuries until they're claimed, or until a certain number of years pass. The important thing to know is that searching for and recovering funds is *free*—so don't fall for scams asking you to pay money to recover assets that you can rightfully claim. NAUPA is a legitimate nonprofit organization representing state treasuries. Visit unclaimed.org to start your search. Also check treasuryhunt.gov for unclaimed savings bonds.

Savings: Per NAUPA, if you're that one-in-eight, an average of **$1,000.**

prised how much great stuff you find along the road!"), and grow most of their own food in what they call their "no-cost garden," a backyard plot where they cultivate crops raised from recycled seeds and cuttings they swap with friends.

Although they do their share of dumpster diving, Anneli and Kristan don't consider themselves Freegans, since they do pay for some of the things they consume and they don't share all of the social and political views associated with Freegans. (Freeganism was born in the 1990s out of the antiglobalization and environmental movements. Freegans believe in leading an anticonsumerist lifestyle, salvaging food and other discarded items from dumpsters and elsewhere for political reasons, rather than out of need.) Anneli and Kristan employ some of the same salvaging techniques in their daily lives, but they do so mostly for personal reasons: to live more simply, reduce their dependency on money, and live lighter on the earth. "It's funny," Anneli told me, "we don't know what anything costs anymore because it's been so long since we've paid for anything."

Life, Liberty, and the Pursuit of Free Stuff

Is dumpster diving—picking stuff out of other people's and businesses's trash—legal?

Believe it or not, the U.S. Supreme Court ruled on the issue, sort of, back in 1988, when the justices had their docket priorities straight. In *California v. Greenwood* the Court held that there is no common-law expectation of privacy for discarded materials. In essence, barring other factors, you're free to go through someone else's trash and take whatever you want.

Although the case dealt with the warrantless search of a suspect's garbage by police, for dumpster divers it's their *Roe v. Wade*, a true landmark ruling. The Court in its majority opinion expressed the view that it is "common knowledge" that garbage at the side of the street is "readily accessible to animals, children, scavengers, snoops, and other members of the public." It's worth noting that while cheapskates were not specifically mentioned, we definitely qualify as a hybrid of animal, scavenger, and snoop.

Even though avid dumpster divers sometimes carry copies of the Supreme Court's ruling with them in order to document their

CHEAP SHOT
COUCHSURFING

Travel the world without having to pay for overnight lodging? CouchSurfing (CouchSurfing.org) is a worldwide, nonprofit network of half a million people who open their homes to fellow travelers, letting you sleep on their couch (or often in a spare bedroom) for the night. Not only is it free, but it's a great way to really *experience* a travel destination. Their robust website includes a system of checks and balances that helps make CouchSurfing safe and ensures a good match between a host and a traveler. You can choose whether to register to host fellow travelers, or just be a surfer. It's not just for single travelers or young people, either; there are user groups for families, senior citizens, you name it. CouchSurfing's motto is "Creating a Better World, One Couch at a Time," and I can tell you from personal experience that it's doing just that.

Savings: Try it even one night instead of a hotel, and you'll probably save **$100** or so.

inalienable right to rummage, they may still not be in the clear all of the time. State and local governments can adopt laws regarding privacy and trash collection that are more restrictive than federal laws, and of course trespassing laws still apply. Know those laws before you dive, and be aware that rules regarding salvaging items at landfills are set by the state or county, so check with your landfill first. Many landfills have designated areas where they set aside usable items that you're free to take home with you.

CHAPTER 8

We Can't Retire. We Went out to Dinner Instead.

As a child my family's menu consisted of two choices:
take it or leave it.
—Buddy Hackett

When I grew up in the 1960s and early '70s, my family, like most families I knew at that time, rarely ate meals prepared outside the home. Dining out in a restaurant—or even springing for Chinese carryout or an occasional Big Mac—was, in and of itself, a special occasion. And in fact such meals were generally reserved for truly special occasions, like birthdays, anniversaries, or a school report card worthy of celebrating. Come to think of it, maybe the rarity of that last occurrence is the reason we ate out so infrequently.

Honestly, I can still vividly remember almost every restaurant or fast-food meal we ate when I was growing up. That's how rare they were.

There was the fortieth wedding anniversary for my Grandpa and Grandma Yeager at the fancy German restaurant in Toledo. That was the first time I ever ate spaetzle. I instantly fell in love with those cute little German dumplings, even though after dinner my brother told me that I'd actually been eating grubworms, which caused me to lose my entire sauerbraten and spaetzle dinner during the drive home.

Whenever I see a Howard Johnson's I still think back to the all-you-can-eat fried clam dinner my parents treated us to when I made second lieutenant of the school safety patrol. Not to brag, but I was the first fourth-grader at Whiteford Road Elementary to ever ascend to that level of safety patrol authority, and I celebrated by consuming one-and-a-half times my body weight in clam strips and tartar sauce.

CHEAP SHOT
WATER DOWN THE CHECK WHEN YOU DINE OUT

Okay, so the touching tales from my childhood haven't convinced you to return to the bygone days when dining out was reserved for special occasions. Take a baby step instead and order only tap water with your meal when you go out to eat. Heck, even ask them to put a piece of lemon in it (aka a Cheapskate Spritzer). Beverages—both alcoholic and otherwise—are typically marked up 300 to 600 percent or more by dining establishments and account for about 20 percent of the average tab for a meal prepared outside the home. If you want to enjoy a glass of wine or cocktail with dinner, have one at home before you go out—provided that you don't overdo it before getting behind the wheel.

Savings: Cutting beverages out of the $4,000 or so the average family of four spends on meals prepared outside the home could save you about $800 a year. Not too shabby for a baby step.

And my lifelong love affair with Chinese food began during a sad time in my young life, after my Grandma Cooper died and my newly, awkwardly widowed grandfather took to ordering chop-suey carryout for us when we came over for dinner. It was the most exotic thing I'd ever eaten, and it made the empty chair at the table a little less painfully noticeable.

Those childhood memories of the rare occasions when we *didn't* eat home-cooked meals came welling up—sort of like that spaetzle, only pleasantly—as I sat around the dining room tables of my fellow cheapskates while writing this book. It was like I'd entered a time warp and returned to 1972, or been inducted into a secret society of folks who only eat meals prepared outside the home when there's something to celebrate or home cooking isn't an option.

What's the Big Deal? It's Only a Happy Meal

If you're looking for the cheapskate next door, don't look in a restaurant or even "fast-food joint," as Grandma Yeager called them. The cheapskates next door report that only about 5 percent of their total spending on food is spent on meals prepared outside the home. That's roughly one-tenth of what the typical American family spends.

According to the U.S. Statistical Abstract, spending on meals other than those prepared at home is now approaching 50 percent of the average family's total food budget. That percentage has been increasing at a rate of about 1/2 to 1 percent per year for the past four decades. The typical U.S. family of four now spends almost $4,000 per year on meals prepared outside the home. Now *that's* a lot of clams, fried or otherwise.

It's also a lot of hamburgers and French fries. A story on PBS

NewsHour Extra claimed that the average American consumes three hamburgers and four orders of fries each week, or an average of 159 fast-food meals each year. If you're a kid growing up today, I kind of doubt that you'll have a childhood memory to keep you company later in life from each of those burger-in-a-sack dining experiences. It's clear that the trend toward eating meals prepared outside the home is driven more by perceived convenience than it is by the desirability or quality of the food itself.

With meals prepared outside the home easily costing three times, four times, or even more times as much as buying the raw ingredients and cooking the same meals at home, a cheapskate family of four saves roughly $3,000 a year by cooking nearly all of its meals at home. Invest that savings as your kids are growing up, and even at a 5-percent rate of return you'll have about $100,000 in their college fund by the time they enroll. College degree or dinners at Denny's: You decide.

But once again, most cheapskates will tell you that the cost savings are at best a secondary consideration; the primary benefit of home cooking is spending time together as a family. "We *always* eat as a family, even if that means waiting until nine o'clock at night for everyone to get home," Paul Kasley, of Hillside, Illinois, told me.

The cheapskates next door practice naturally what a recent article in the *Archives of Pediatrics & Adolescent Medicine* prescribed. Frequent family meals, it confirmed, are associated with a lower risk of smoking, drinking, and using marijuana among adolescents; lower incidents of depression; and better grades in school. A number of cheapskate parents have added that limiting restaurant meals and carryout food—meals at which kids pick and choose off a menu—has helped make their children less finicky about what they eat.

CHEAP SHOT
GO ONLINE BEFORE YOU DINE

As for those special occasions when the cheapskates next door do go out for dinner, time and again they told me that they always check out Restaurant.com beforehand, where they buy a discounted "gift certificate" to use at a participating restaurant. Typically a $25 certificate on the popular website sells for $10, so you save $15 off your dinner tab. But there are often special promotional offers available through which you can buy a $25 certificate on Restaurant.com for as little as $2, saving you a whopping $23 on dinner. To find special deals on certificates, Google "promotion code restaurant.com." You need to register with the website—it's free—before you can purchase certificates, and terms and conditions vary depending on the restaurant, so read the details carefully. That said, it really is a terrific way to save, and since you're redeeming a "gift certificate" it removes the social stigma some feel when using a regular coupon.

Savings: Variable, but I recently paid only $8 for $100 in gift certificates for our favorite local Greek restaurant for a savings of $92.

Try It the Cheapskate Way

The key to slashing what you spend on meals prepared outside the home is to make dining out—or even grabbing carryout—*less convenient* than eating meals prepared at home. It's another case of good habits being hard to break, and making sure the path of least resistance happens to be the one that also saves you the most. "If eating at home is the easiest option, it's not a sacrifice, is it?" Donna Rodgers told me.

The secret, according to the cheapskates next door, is to cook meals in batches (see Chapter 11) and make sure you always have plenty of easy, ready-to-eat items on hand, like sandwich supplies, snack items, and fresh fruit. Cultivating an interest in cooking obviously helps, too, when it comes to steering you toward preparing more meals at home; about 80 percent of cheapskates reported having a moderate or stronger interest in cooking. Borrowing cookbooks from the library and watching cooking shows on TV can help to spark an interest in cooking, even among reluctant chefs.

And when cheapskates do dine out, they frequently order in a style I call "à la cheap," as opposed to "à la carte." Splitting entrées or ordering off the appetizer menu not only helps prevent sticker shock when the check arrives, it also helps to counteract the trend toward super-sized portions that has afflicted most dining establishments these days. Jean Chapman, of Fuquay Varina, North Carolina, writes that when she and her husband dine out, "We order one entrée and a side salad and share both . . . It keeps our weight down and also our budget."

Restaurant servings of steak, for example, are often twelve ounces or even larger, whereas government dietary guidelines suggest a three-ounce serving. Restaurants frequently serve one to two cups of pasta per diner, when a recommended portion is just half a cup. A study by the NPD Group, a market research firm, found that the typical American restaurant meal has about 60 percent more calories than the average meal made at home. That's a coincidence: According to the American Obesity Association, about 60 percent of Americans are also overweight. Go figure.

The à la cheap restaurant menu also features Cheapskate Spritzers to drink (see Cheap Shot) and includes dessert—only it's waiting for you at home. Another favorite cheapskate tradition is having a simple appetizer at home, *before* you go out for dinner. Even if it's just a slice of whole-grain bread dipped in olive oil or some cheese and crackers, it helps to curb your appetite—and bill—at the restaurant. And younger cheapskates often go a different route, making an entire meal out of the free hors d'oeuvres

---

CHEAP SHOT
TOO BUSY TO PACK A LUNCH? PACK A BIG BROWN BAG JUST ONCE A WEEK

Sure, you've heard it before. *Save big money by brown bagging your lunch.* But who has time to pack a lunch every day? I know I never did when I was an office jockey. Then one day I had an economic epiphany: Rather than make my lunch at home and carry it into the office every day, why not just carry a bag of groceries to the office once a week and make my lunches there? From then on, I rarely went out to lunch. The quickest, most convenient (not to mention cheapest) solution when my stomach started to grumble at lunchtime was the loaf of pumpernickel stashed in my file cabinet and the assortment of cold cuts and fresh fruits and veggies with my name on them in the office fridge. Heck, even if you need to buy your own mini-fridge for the office or cooler for the job site, I bet you'll come out ahead in just the first month or two.

Savings: Say $4 per work day, *$1,000 a year* . . . or about **$40,000** over the course of a typical career.

offered at some bars during happy hour, or seeking out restaurants where it's okay to bring your own bottle of wine.

Of course, when the cheapskates next door dine out, they frequently stretch their dollars by using a coupon, like those from the popular website Restaurant.com (see Cheap Shot), the Entertainment Books (entertainment.com), local newspapers, or the chamber of commerce.

One of my Miser Advisers from New York City also has a great tip for scoring half-price gourmet carryout for dinner. She writes that gourmet "lunch bars" in the city, which sell food by the pound, frequently cut their prices in half in the late afternoon, once the lunch rush is over. I took her advice and have found that similar dining establishments in other cities sometimes do the same thing.

A final fact that probably won't surprise you and another one that probably will: More than 90 percent of cheapskates routinely ask for a doggy bag when they dine out, and more than 90 percent also report tipping 15 percent or more (on the total, pre-coupon amount) for restaurant service. We're frugal, but we're fair.

CHAPTER 9

The Joys of Horse Trading

Sure. But it'll cost ya'.
—The Ultimate Cheapskate's counteroffer to a lady
of questionable repute in Times Square, who once
asked him, "Hey, big fella', wanna have a good time?"
(Needless to say, the deal was never consummated.)

With dollars stretched tighter than a drumhead these days, the cheapskates next door are leading the way back to the future, returning to the time-honored traditions of both haggling and bartering to get what they need for less. And once again, it's not just about saving a buck.

"Sure, there's a challenge to it. At first I was real nervous," cheapskate Janet Bellows says about her passion for both bartering and negotiating. "That's what makes it a butt-load of fun. I've had a lot of laughs and met a lot of neat people because of it." Most of the cheapskates who engage in haggling and/or bartering on a regular basis share a similar feeling. It's as much about the thrill of the hunt and livening up the typically humdrum retail process as it is about the money.

Let's Make a Deal: It Pays to Haggle

Other than the oft-despised process of buying a new car, Americans don't have a tradition of haggling like that savored by many other cultures around the globe. We're usually shy about asking for a better price on something, or we consider it rude or offensive behavior.

That's too bad, because like bartering, attempting to negotiate a better deal on things can often be kind of fun and save you some serious bucks. A 2007 survey by the Consumer Reports National Research Center found that more than 90 percent of those who got up the nerve to negotiate on things like electronics, appliances, furniture, and even medical bills reported receiving a discount at least once during the survey period, with most saving $50 or more each time they were successful.

The cheapskates next door who are into haggling have plenty of practical advice to share:

RULE #1: Nice guys finish first. Don't be a schmuck. Always be friendly and polite when asking for a better price. As I discussed in my first book, I often ask for (and receive) a "Nice Guy Discount"—a discount based simply on the fact that I'm a nice guy.

RULE #2: Speak to the right person. An increasing number of frontline employees at places like banks, catalog companies, and even large retailers are being empowered by their employers to negotiate with customers to keep us happy or even to make a sale, but sometimes you still need to ask to speak to a supervisor or manager.

RULE #3: Be honest, but don't be shy. Don't fabricate or exaggerate, but politely speak your mind if you're dissatisfied with the service you've received or the quality of a product; it may very likely get you a discount or other perks.

RULE #4: "I can't afford it." Particularly in this economic climate, these are the four most important words you can say.

Whether you're calling to cancel or renew your phone, cable, or some other service, or reacting to the price quoted by a store salesman, this self-confession will often prompt them to sharpen their pencils.

RULE #5: Cheaper by the dozen. Regarding quantity discounts, negotiate the best price for a single item and *then* reveal that you're interested in buying more than one; the per-unit price should drop even more.

RULE #6: Watch for sales *before and after* you buy. Many retailers will give you the sale price or match a competitor's sale price, even if the item you're interested in isn't on sale at the time. Some will even refund the difference after the fact.

RULE #7: Show them the money. Paying with cash instead of a credit card can often get you a better price, since vendors typically pay a couple-percent processing fee on credit card transactions.

RULE #8: Don't sell yourself short by naming a price. Let the salesman name his price first. Don't tell him what you're willing to pay; ask him what he's willing to take. He might start with an even lower price than you would have proposed. Once he's given you a price, you know that's just his starting point, so politely push back and ask him to do even better.

RULE #9: Be careful about threatening. Threatening to "take your business elsewhere" can be an effective negotiating tactic in some situations, but tread softly. It can backfire and turn off the other party if it's viewed as a hollow threat or simply mean-spirited. Be prepared to walk away empty-handed, even if you're bluffing.

RULE #10: "I'd like to cancel my service." Keeping in mind Rule #9, in phone transactions, asking to cancel your service (e.g., cable service, phone plans, credit cards, etc.) will often put you in touch with special personnel who can cut you a better deal to keep you on board.

RULE #11: Never on a Monday. Not so much for retail price haggling but for negotiating in general, in my experience the best deals are made late in the week, particularly on Fridays and especially before holidays or three-day weekends. Everyone's in a good mood and wants to wrap things up. Avoid negotiating early in the week.

RULE #12: If you're still shy about haggling for a better price . . . at least take a baby step by always asking if you're eligible for a discount based on memberships like AARP, AAA, membership warehouse clubs, etc. Even if a merchant doesn't normally honor such memberships, sometimes the fact that you asked will prompt them to knock something off.

Bartering Basics

Bartering—swapping goods and services rather than paying for them—has made a major comeback in the tightening economy and with the proliferation of online barter clubs and websites. Since the economic downturn began, Craigslist.org reported that ads for bartering are among the fastest-growing listings on their sites.

Online barter clubs, like BarterBart.com and uSwapit.com, help facilitate trading. Some barter sites allow users to trade goods and services for credits instead of actual stuff, thereby increasing trading flexibility. Credits can be redeemed at any time for the goods and services you want, rather than depending on finding a swapping partner who just happens to be looking for what you have to offer, when you have it to offer.

Specialty bartering websites are popping up on the Internet like cheapskates at a going-out-of-business sale. Your can swap

CHEAP SHOT
AN INSIDER'S GUIDE TO
CATALOG SAVINGS

It pays to have friends on the inside, and Andrea Bahr, one of my Miser Advisers, is just that. Andrea works for a catalog company and gave me the 411 on some haggling strategies that just might score you some savings the next time you order something over the phone. For instance, if an item is on back order, "mention the word 'cancel' and see how quickly you're offered a discount," Andrea says. Also, always ask if there are any special "promotions" that may apply, since many times there are discount offers that may be available, but operators can only tell you about them if you ask first. The same is true of shipping discounts, so ask specifically about those as well. And if you receive an item and aren't satisfied, just call and mention the possibility of "returning it for a refund" and see if they don't rush to offer you a partial refund or other perk like a gift certificate to keep you from returning your order.

Savings: Variable, but by following Andrea's insider advice, my wife and I have saved more than $80 this past year on our catalog orders.

books at sites like PaperBackSwap.com and BookMooch.com, trade kids' stuff at Kizoodle.com and TotsSwapShop.com, and swap just about everything else at U-Exchange.com. You can trade clothes, shoes, accessories, and even cosmetics at Swapstyle.com, and Swaptree.com specializes in music, DVD, book, and video game trading. And there are even adult sites like wifeswap.com, a virtual version of the old "key parties" back in the 1970s—who knew?

Some of the more creative swaps reported by my fellow cheap-skates include bartering website-design services for home brewing lessons and supplies, wedding photography for house painting, and homemade tomato juice for haircuts. As Miser Adviser Beth Holovach says about that last swap, "Guess that tells you how good my juice is!"

Old-fashioned face-to-face swap meets are a great place to catch the bartering bug and hone your horse-trading skills. You can find swap meets near you at Listingfleamarket.com. Admission

CHEAP SHOT
BARTERING YOUR TIME

No matter what your skills—or lack of skills—may be, there's a growing movement online and in communities across the country to help you trade your time for the services and goods you need, all without the exchange of money. "Time banking" (timebanks.org) is sort of like volunteering with a direct payback. For every hour you spend doing something for somebody in your community, you earn a Time Dollar, which can then be "spent" on having someone do something for you. And at Favorpals.com, you can swap your time walking dogs or washing cars, for example, for child care or professional services like tax preparation, or even for merchandise. Favorpals' motto is "Imagine a world where you can get anything you want by simply giving something in return." I like the way that sounds.

Savings: Swap just an hour or two of your time each week for a year, and you could be the recipient of **$500–$1,000** of free services/goods in return.

to most swap meets is low-cost or even free, so it's also a fun, inexpensive outing for the whole family.

While bartering can be a blast—a chance to score the stuff you want without plunking down a single dead president—be aware of some possible pitfalls. Check merchandise carefully and confirm services in writing before agreeing to a swap, because if you're dissatisfied, recourse can be difficult. Also, turn over merchandise *after* the agreed-upon services have been provided, or swap goods/services simultaneously so you don't come up empty-handed.

The Bartering Tax Morass

So bartering is back—and thanks to the Internet it's bigger than ever—but is bartering legal? "I'm amazed how often this question is asked," says John Moore, owner of the bartering website U-Exchange.com. He adds, "The only thing that is not legal is failing to claim bartering on your taxes." Simple enough.

Guess again. The official explanation is that barter trades are generally treated the same as cash transactions and are reported on Form 1040, Schedule C, *Profit or Loss from Business.* That's right: If you engage in bartering, in the eyes of the IRS you're generally considered to be in business.

But the IRS agent I spoke with over the phone had all the self-confidence of a squirrel crossing a busy street when attempting to explain to me the tax implications of the specific, real-life examples of bartering I presented. It quickly became dizzyingly complicated, leading me to understand why many of the bartering enthusiasts I spoke with hinted that tax reporting was not one of their top priorities. Even the IRS agent conceded that many bartering transactions, particularly informal exchanges between individuals, are going unreported.

Tim Kelly, partner at the Atlanta-based accounting firm Bennett Thrasher, says, "In order to determine whether a taxable event has occurred, mentally reduce the transaction to cash and test whether that exchange would require tax reporting." Gross income from all sources is generally considered taxable, and that includes income from barter transactions based on the fair market value (FMV) of goods and services exchanged.

For example, if two individuals exchange used items of approximately equal value, the transaction is not likely to require tax reporting, provided that the items have decreased in value since originally acquired; it's the same as if you simply sold a used item at a yard sale. However, if one or both of the items have appreciated in value, then capital gains tax is probably due. There always seems to be a catch.

But let's say a retired attorney agrees to draw up your will in exchange for use of your summer cottage for a couple of days. According to Kelly, the attorney may be required to report the FMV of the summer cottage stay as income, although you would not normally report the transaction on your taxes, since you "paid" for the service, just not with cash. Of course, he adds, that's provided that you don't rent or barter use of your cottage for more than fourteen days each year, in which case it generally would be taxable. See how simple?

While some might try to disguise such bartering exchanges as gifts (gifts under $12,000 are generally nontaxable), that won't fly if there's an expectation that something will be given back in return.

Thankfully, at least some rules of reason apply, says Kelly. "If you drive me to the coffee shop and I buy the coffee for both of us, the IRS isn't likely to start an examination, presuming each action was a 'gift' made without expectation of a return." Well, that's reassuring to know.

The bottom line: Consult IRS Publication 525—and a qualified tax professional—to better understand the tax consequences of your specific bartering activities.

Cheapskates Speak

- **"I was in the market for a new sewing machine,"** says Glyndalyn Willard, bemoaning the demise of her beloved Singer after twenty-eight years of faithful service. "I called a dealer in Nashville, and they had the one I wanted and quoted me a price. I went to see them armed with cash. The machine was what I wanted and I offered them $200 less than the price they quoted me. While making the offer, I took the cash out of my purse and laid it down where the seller could see it. They took the offer so quickly I wish I had offered less!"

- **"My husband is a very handy man, which is one of the reasons I married him,"** confesses Cassy Lynn. "He exchanges work on heating and air-conditioning for haircuts with his barber. His hair is really getting long, so I have been telling him to get over there and get to work on the AC!"

- **Even medical expenses are sometimes negotiable,** as my fellow cheapskate Carol Simpson found out. Left waiting in the exam room for forty-five minutes, Carol voiced her displeasure and the $100 fee for the visit was waived. "I just politely explained to the doctor that my time was just as important to me as his was to him, and I showed up on time." Particularly if you're uninsured, always ask the medical provider for a discount. They often charge different fees, depending on who's paying—you, or an insurance company.

- **"They need you more than you need them!"** says Miser Adviser John L. Hoh, Jr., explaining how he has saved hundreds of dollars on magazine and newspaper subscriptions over the years. "Publishers make their money on advertising [not subscription fees], and they set their ad rates based on the number of subscribers they have." Knowing this, John routinely asks to speak to a manager in the subscription department, and tells him that he'll only subscribe (or renew) if they knock down his subscription rate to a bare minimum.

CHEAP SHOT
AND NOW I LAY ME DOWN FOR CHEAP: NEGOTIATING YOUR OWN FUNERAL EXPENSES

Last—but hardly least—even your final expenses may be negotiable. Don't be shy about comparison shopping and leveraging one offer against the other for burial plots, headstones, and other funeral services; but don't be suckered in by pre-need funeral packages, which are often a notorious rip-off. For the biggest savings, choose "direct cremation" and consider a rental or cardboard casket (just Google 'em). And always remember: *You're in a much better negotiating position while you're still in a vertical position!* Make your funeral plans and wishes known while you're still living, and don't leave the negotiation of your final arrangements to grief-stricken—and therefore vulnerable—family members.

Savings: Shave even 10 percent off the cost of the average U.S. funeral, and you'll RIP a little easier with a $650–$1,000 savings (of course that's a once-in-a-lifetime savings, so to speak).

- **Banking services is another very competitive industry,** and therefore ripe for haggling. My cheapskate confidante Barbie King of Dunedin, Florida, reported a not-uncommon story. Barbie (aka "The Black Belt Tightwad") got a hefty $39 bank fee waived simply by asking the friendly bank manager if she could make an exception. Banking is one of many industries where even clerks and other frontline employees are increasingly being empowered to do whatever's necessary to keep you as a happy customer.

CHAPTER 10

Break the Mortgage Chains that Bind Thee

A mortgage is a house with a guilty conscience.
—Exact source unknown, but no doubt
some cheapskate next door

I've already told you a little bit about some of the more interesting cheapskate homes I've had a chance to visit, like Jacquie Phelan's "Taj Mahovel" and the house that Kate Easlick got for free in the rolling hills of northern Michigan.

Then there's Becka and Justin Miller, who live in Baltimore—or, rather, Baltimore Harbor. The recently married young couple lives "on the hook," as they say in nautical circles, having bought a forty-eight-foot steel-hulled sailing ship—still afloat but showing its years—as their first home. At a mere $18,000, they couldn't pass up such a deal, even if it (or is that "she?") spends most of the time dockside and they spend most of their free time happily keeping it/her seaworthy and making their ship into their home.

"It's not just a place to live, it's an adventure," they told me. "We don't have much space (less than 500 square feet, including usable outside deck space), but we find that living in a small space puts us at peace with what we have, who we are, and where we live."

There's no denying the fact that many cheapskates—myself and my wife included—have a passion for eclectic housing. Part of it is a money thing; nontraditional housing often costs less, sometimes a lot less. But I suspect that for most of us it's more about expressing and being comfortable with who we are.

We want to live in a place that is truly *our home*, not a house that we buy to keep up social appearances, or just because it's a good investment, or a home that we're afraid to modify to fit our

---

CHEAP SHOT
LOCATION, LOCATION, LOCATION

Until gas prices got so high that they started giving us octane-induced nosebleeds, most Americans apparently didn't think too much about the financial cost of a long daily commute. For decades, when gas was cheap, the proximity of our home to our place of employment wasn't unimportant, but it was more a question of how much time—not how much money—our daily commute would cost us. That mindset led us to the situation today, where, according to an ABC News report, the average American commutes about sixteen miles a day, *each way*, to his/her job. Given that the AAA estimates that it costs about fifty cents to drive the typical car one mile (including the cost of depreciation, gas, insurance, maintenance, etc.), that means the typical U.S. commute costs about $4,000 per year. Live closer to where you work, and save big-time.

Savings: Consider this: If you lived close enough to walk to work to save that **$4,000** per year, and invested it at a 5-percent rate of return, over a forty-year career you'd have a nest egg of **$535,519.01** to show for it (plus a terrific-looking pair of legs, I'd bet).

particular (peculiar?) tastes for fear of negatively impacting its all-important "resale value." We want the luxury of owning a home that's about *us*, not about what other people have or want or think. Ironically, that kind of housing often costs less than traditional housing.

None of this is to say that all cheapskates live in funky places. If you were to visit the very comfortable, nicely appointed homes of cheapskates like Gerald and Julie Thomson, or Bruce Ostyn and Daniel Newman, or Kelly Kamann, you'd never know that you'd entered the abode of a cheapskate next door. They own traditional-style homes, in pleasant neighborhoods, and they don't even have to worry about bilge pumps and barnacle cuts, like you do when you're living on the hook.

Bucking Three-Home Ownership Trends

Style aside, the cheapskates next door have plenty in common when it comes to their homes.

First, they tend to buy smaller homes than the typical American, or at least the typical American these days. Homes of the cheapskates polled averaged roughly 1,650 square feet, well below the national average of about 2,300 square feet. Like most Americans once did, the cheapskates next door buy "right-sized" homes, when the trend all around them has been to buy "super-sized" homes.

At 1,650 square feet, they're living in homes whose size was the norm back in the late 1970s, which I don't recall as being uncomfortably small (although, in the interest of full disclosure, there are a number of aspects of the late 1970s that I do not recall at all).

This means that in many instances they're living in older homes too, since the average new home built in the United States in 2007 topped out at over 2,500 square feet. As I noted in my first book, the cost of U.S. housing per square foot has increased only by roughly the rate of inflation since the 1950s, but we spend almost double (in inflation-adjusted dollars) on housing today than what we did in the '50s, simply because most Americans now want twice as much house.

Secondly, the cheapskates next door tend to buy homes that cost less than what they could qualify to buy based on their income. The cheapskates next door are truly "under-buyers" when they go house hunting. While *the times they are a-changing* since the burst of the housing bubble, for years mortgage lenders would allow you to borrow (well, more accurately, "encourage" you to borrow) up to three times or even more of your gross annual household income to buy a new home. A whole lot of folks went right out and spent every penny they could qualify for on their new castle.

To the cheapskates next door, what they can "qualify" to borrow isn't the issue. It's how much they feel they can *afford* to spend, which is usually far less than the amount the lender is willing to allow them to borrow. A number of cheapskates indicated that they try to keep their housing costs (mortgage payments, taxes, insurance, maintenance) to 25 or 30 percent of their take-home pay, resulting in a house costing only about two-thirds as much as what they could probably qualify to buy. Some of the two-income cheapskate families I spoke with determined the amount they felt comfortable spending on a house using only one of their two incomes in the calculation, wisely making sure that they could continue to meet their mortgage payments if one spouse lost a job.

And finally, the cheapskates next door are vigilant about paying off their homes as quickly as possible, whether it's a ranch-style home in a leafy subdivision or a steel-hulled scow bobbing around in Baltimore Harbor. Of the cheapskate homeowners polled, more

CHEAP SHOT
HOME IMPROVEMENTS: TIMING IS EVERYTHING

While many cheapskates thrive on doing most or all of their home repairs and improvements themselves, some are less keen on do-it-yourself projects around the house. "In the end it would cost twice as much if I tried to fix it myself. First the repairman would have to repair the original problem, then repair the additional damage I did trying to 'fix' it myself," cheapskate Don Gillette, a self-confessed "un-handyman," said. When hiring out home projects, the cheapskates next door know that good timing can save big money. Find out the "slow seasons" for various home service providers, as you're likely to pay less by scheduling your job during that time. For example: Tree services and landscapers are often hurting for work in the wintertime. Schedule exterior home repairs in the fall and winter, and interior jobs in the spring and summer. Get your lawn mower tuned up in the winter, your chimney swept in the summer, and your carpets cleaned *after* the holidays. It can be cheaper to hire a moving company between October and April than during the busy summer months, if that fits into your relocation plans.

Savings: Variable, but one cheapskate saved 30 percent—a whopping $650—by having his new outdoor deck built during the winter instead of the summer.

than 80 percent said they plan to pay off their mortgages early or already have. As mentioned previously, this is in stark contrast to the general U.S. population, given that more than half of all Americans will go to their graves still owing on a home mortgage and/or debt secured against their homes.

They're Just Like You, and They're Doing It Every Day

I'm not going to repeat the detailed information contained in my first book about how to pay off your home mortgage early, or the multitude of reasons why you should do it. All of that advice and information, based on the strategies my wife and I used to pay off our home in only sixteen years while earning relatively modest salaries, remains as true today as it did when I wrote it. What's more, since then, that advice has been reaffirmed time and again by the cheapskates next door, and they have proven that it's possible to pay off your home early regardless of your family situation.

Single homeowners like Bruce Jackson are successfully paying off their mortgages early, or already have, often on relatively modest salaries. Bruce paid off his home in only eight years, in part because he bought a duplex and rents out the other half. He was able to retire at age thirty-nine after spending just fifteen years as a bank officer. He's also one of the few cheapskates next door I've encountered who owns a "vacation home," albeit a 192-square-foot cabin in Vermont, without electricity or running water (although it does feature a wood-fired outside bathtub). Bruce says it's a great place to lead a simple life—and have a good soak, alfresco style.

Married homeowners, both with and without children, are paying off their mortgages early, too—again, sometimes on modest salaries and/or a single income. Danny Kofke supports his family of four on a schoolteacher's salary of approximately $40,000 a year, and he'll have their home paid off in a total of just nineteen years, at the most. The Kofkes bought a house "below their means" and soon refinanced a thirty-year mortgage to take advantage of lower rates and trim the term to just twenty years, which they're paying down even faster with additional payments to principal. "We have been very content in a relatively smaller house. The more space you have, the more stuff you buy to fill that space," he said.

If the cheapskates next door can do it, you can do it too. You can break the mortgage chains that bind thee. It's not easy—it takes discipline and focus—but it is possible and it gets more and more rewarding as you go along. Here are the key points:

1. Buy less house than you can afford. Ask the lender how large a mortgage you can qualify for, and then go hunting for a house priced at no more than 75 percent of that amount (and hopefully closer to 50 percent).

2. Stay in that house as long as you can. Enjoy it. Make it your own. Put down roots. Get to know your neighbors (particularly the cheapskates next door).

3. Make additional payments toward principal whenever possible. Maybe it's just a few extra dollars at first, or the proceeds from a yard sale or some extra overtime pay. Small payments toward principal add up to big savings on interest over the course of the loan.

4. This is a biggie: Whenever you get a pay raise, allocate most or all of your increase toward paying off your mort-

gage early. That's when the mortgage really starts to melt away.

5. Consider setting up a "mortgage acceleration plan" with your lender. These plans typically involve making a partial mortgage payment every two weeks, equal to roughly one-half of your current monthly payment. By making twenty-six biweekly payments, you are in essence making an extra monthly payment each year. Most mortgage lenders offer such plans for free, and they'll knock years and many thousands of dollars in interest off your existing mortgage—and it's fairly painless, too.

6. If you refinance to take advantage of lower interest rates, do the math carefully and shorten—never lengthen—the remaining term of the loan. For example, if you've already paid for ten years on a thirty-year mortgage and want to refinance because interest rates have gone down, whatever you do, *don't* set the clock back again by taking out a new thirty-year mortgage. Consider setting the clock forward instead, and see if you can swing a new fifteen-year mortgage at the lower interest rate; it's probably a lot more doable than you think, and you'll cut the mortgage chains that bind thee five years sooner.

7. Most important of all, keep your eye on the prize. Become one of the few, the proud, the well rested—an American who actually owns his house free and clear. Don't be envious of your neighbors if they move on to bigger, more expensive homes. What they're really moving on to is a bigger, more expensive mortgage, higher taxes and expenses, and years and years more of living under the yoke of debt.

CHEAP SHOT
GUERRILLA GARDENING—LANDSCAPING ON THE CHEAP

Gardening and landscaping are favorite pastimes among the cheapskates next door, and a well-landscaped yard can significantly increase the value of your home and even reduce your energy bills. According to the U.S. Department of Energy (energy.gov), as few as three strategically planted trees in your yard can lower your heating and cooling costs by up to 25 percent. But the cheapskates next door aren't spending a fortune on plants and other landscaping materials; they're into *guerrilla gardening* instead.

They swap plants with friends and neighbors and at plant-swap meets (see plantswap.net), and they befriend local landscapers who often discard plants they uproot from landscaping jobs. They divide and propagate more plants from the plants they already own. They score free or cheap mulch from the local highway department or landfill. They get creative and recycle everything, from old tires and soda bottles to bed frames and bowling balls, into one-of-a-kind garden art.

Savings: Variable, but one cheapskate told me she swapped some of her hosta plants with a neighbor who was long on English ivy and saved more than $100.

Whenever I meet someone who advises against paying off a mortgage early—and, trust me, I meet them on an almost daily basis—I always ask them if they've experienced, firsthand, the sense of freedom and exhilaration that comes from being mortgage free. Have they in fact ever paid off a mortgage of their own?

To date, not a single such person has responded in the affirmative. Until that day comes, I rest my case.

CHAPTER 11

Bon Appe-cheap!
Come on into the Cheapskate's Kitchen

Sex is good, but not as good as fresh, sweet corn.
—Garrison Keillor

I love to cook, almost as much as I love to eat. My mother not only taught me how to cook at a young age, but she somehow instilled in me a lifelong passion for the culinary arts, albeit culinary arts cheapskate style. I can't begin to calculate how much money I've saved on restaurant meals over the years by virtue of the fact that, most of all, I love to cook and eat at home.

What I didn't learn from Mom, I picked up from piles of cookbooks borrowed from the public library and cooking shows on PBS. Growing up, I loved the naughty-boy kitchen antics of Graham Kerr on *The Galloping Gourmet*. Later, the delicious-but-economical recipes of Jeff Smith, aka *The Frugal Gourmet*, really excited not only my taste buds but my emerging Inner Miser.

But none will ever compare with my beloved Julia Child—despite the memorable embarrassment I suffered the first time I ever saw Julia's show on TV.

Growing up, before I'd ever heard of *The French Chef*, my mischievous older brother, Joel, told me that "bon appetit" was French slang meant to belittle the size of one's manly apparatus. Not speaking French, I accepted this definition as an article of faith (not based on any personal anatomical truth, mind you), and I frequently used the phrase to put down guys who bullied me in gym class. It was so cutting, yet so sophisticated.

Coach Sacstretcher even asked me one day what it meant. When I told him, he chuckled and said, "Cool! Now I can tell all the ladies I speak French" (or *Franch*, as he pronounced it). Shortly thereafter I noticed that Sacstretcher started wearing a beret to school, which was the only one ever seen to this day in Tontogany, Ohio.

So you can imagine my mortification the first time I sat down in front of our black and white Motorola TV set, the one with the limed wood finish, and tuned in to *The French Chef* with Julia Child. I immediately fell in love with Child's gregarious style and delightful accent. I still remember what she cooked that day: a rosemary-crusted leg of lamb with oven-roasted potatoes and braised Belgium endive.

And then it happened. At the end of the show, standing proudly behind her beautifully carved leg of lamb, Julia looked straight into the camera—straight into my eyes—and announced to the world, "Bon appetit!"—or, as I heard it, *You have a little boner!*

It took several minutes for me to comprehend the cruel delusion I'd been living under. When I finally tracked down Joel, he howled with laughter and chanted "Bon appetit! Bon appetit! Bon appetit!" as he pranced around the living room, fending off my seventh-grade punches.

The Three Great Grocery Debates

Grocery shopping brings out the competitive streak in the cheapskate next door. I suppose that's because almost everyone needs to shop for food; it's sort of the ultimate proving ground for one's thrift-craft. And there's no shortage of opinions among cheapskates when it comes to different grocery shopping strategies, as we'll see in a minute. Nonetheless, through a variety of different-but-effective methods, the cheapskate next door is spending a lot less on groceries than most Americans.

The average American family of four spends close to $9,000 per year on groceries, or about $2,250 per person, per year. The average spent by those cheapskates I surveyed was more than 40 percent less, or roughly $1,300 per person, a savings of nearly $1,000 per person, per year. Of course, individual spending depends a great deal on the size of the family (grocery costs per person tend to decrease as the size of the family increases), region of the country, and other factors.

There is no single secret for reducing your family's grocery bill for that kind of savings, but there are a number of distinct—and sometime contrary—strategies, one or more of which will certainly work for you. These competing strategies are the subject of what I call *The Three Great Grocery Debates*.

The Stockpiler vs. the Spontaneous Chef

There are two basic breeds of cheapskate grocery shoppers: the *stockpiler* and the *spontaneous chef*. Certainly neither approach is at the total exclusion of the other. A stockpiler can also be a spontaneous chef, and the other way around. But in my experience with cheapskates, most of us tend to fall primarily into one category or the other.

The stockpiler is the most common type of cheapskate grocery shopper. Stockpilers don't go out and buy what they need when they need it, but rather buy what's on sale, and save it until they're ready to use it. Stockpilers usually own a large stand-alone freezer and have ample pantry space to store their surplus provisions.

"When people look in my grocery cart, they think I'm crazy," one stockpiler told me. "I'll have twelve jars of pasta sauce (because it's on sale and keeps for an eternity), and not a single box of pasta."

Menu planning for the stockpiler is largely a matter of *taking inventory*, looking at what they already have on hand and perhaps augmenting it with some perishable items they pick up from the store on a weekly basis. Both stockpilers and spontaneous chefs plan their menus ahead of time, before they shop, but stockpilers often plan their menus over a number of weeks or even a month. Obviously the risk you run with stockpiling is the potential of spoilage, but practice and good organization can mitigate that.

Spontaneous chefs are cheapskates who have the culinary interest and ability to creatively transform the ingredients they have at hand—or what's on sale at any given time—into scrumptious meals at the drop of a spatula. Spontaneous chefs tend to have fewer foods on hand, in their pantries or freezers, and they cook more often using fresh ingredients. As a spontaneous chef myself, I wrote a lot about this approach to grocery shopping and cooking in my first book, including my somewhat controversial claim that if you're a smart shopper and creative cook you can cook healthy, delicious meals using only ingredients that cost under one dollar per pound.

Spontaneous chefs frequently are folks who truly love to cook, and about a third of the cheapskates I polled greatly enjoy cooking. "For me, cooking is one of the greatest joys in life," cheapskate Becky Connor told me. "It's so rewarding to know that you made this meal yourself, and think about how much more it would have cost you in a restaurant."

For the spontaneous chef, their menu for the week—or at least the list of ingredients they have to work with—usually arrives on their doorstep in the form of the weekly sales circulars from the local supermarket(s). These contain the so-called "loss leaders" (items that stores sell at a loss or at least a very steep discount in order to get you into the store), around which the spontaneous chef plans his meals for the week. Loss leaders are normally featured prominently on the front page of the store circulars, and increasingly require the use of a store "loyalty card" (usually free) in order to get the sale price. For spontaneous chef wannabes, websites like Epicurious.com provide plenty of recipes based on whatever loss-leader ingredients you have to work with.

Membership Warehouse Stores vs. Supermarkets

"I went in for some hot dogs, and walked out with a hot tub."

Yeah, that can happen if you're prone to impulse buying and you shop at membership warehouse stores like Sam's Club, Costco, and BJ's Wholesale Club. The stakes are so much higher. If you give in to temptation at a regular grocery store, you might end up splurging on a half gallon of ice cream that wasn't on your shopping list; but at a membership warehouse store, it might be a $200 gelato machine.

The cheapskates next door are divided—and plenty opinionated—when it comes to shopping at membership warehouse stores. Roughly half of those polled say they do, and half say they don't.

Some cheapskates, particularly those with large families, say they do their grocery shopping almost exclusively at warehouse stores. "When you have six kids, you don't have a lot of time to shop. At Costco I know I'm at least getting a decent price . . . The large quantities cut down on the number of shopping trips," one cheapskate mom told me.

Others say there are no true bargains to be had at warehouse stores and so, almost as a matter of principle, they never set foot in such places. "We refuse to pay for the privilege of shopping," Daniel Newman and Bruce Ostyn told me in unison, referring to the annual membership fees charged by most warehouse stores.

The facts are these: Membership warehouse stores undeniably have better-than-average prices on a great many items; but for a cheapskate shopper willing to take the time and find the deals, warehouse stores rarely have the *best* prices on groceries and other items. Shopping the loss leaders at grocery stores—aka "cherry picking"—with or without coupons (which are sometimes not redeemable at warehouse stores) is widely accepted as the best way to score the absolutely lowest prices on groceries.

But that doesn't mean membership warehouse stores are a bad place to shop, or that you shouldn't consider shopping there. It's certainly possible to pay a lot more at many grocery stores than you'll pay at a warehouse store. It largely depends on your lifestyle, family size, shopping and cooking habits, storage capacity, and your proximity to the nearest warehouse store.

Assuming that you've vaccinated yourself against impulse buying, the downsides of shopping at a warehouse store are the large quantities/packaging of many items (and related storage and spoilage issues) and the annual membership fees, which you need to remember to factor into the cost. The upsides are generally reasonable prices, fewer trips to the store because of the large quantities, and, in some cases, higher-quality "restaurant-grade" meats and produce you can't find at most bargain-priced supermarkets.

The Couponeers vs. the Coupon Critics

To clip or not to clip, that is the question. There is no single issue that divides the cheapskate population more than couponing. Roughly one-third of those polled swear by the use of coupons;

one-third vehemently opposes the use of coupons; and the last third say they occasionally use coupons. It's like the Civil War out there, only there are three sides and it's even bloodier.

Cheapskates who are serious about using coupons are *really* serious about it. They scour the Sunday newspaper with scissors in hand, swap coupons with friends and neighbors, and download coupons online from websites like CouponBug.com, TheGrocery Game.com, and CouponMom.com (see Cheap Shot). They live for double and rarified triple-coupon days offered by some supermarkets, and they go berserk whenever there's a chance to "pair" or "layer" coupons with store specials and other deals. Another popular couponing strategy is to buy the smallest (i.e., least expensive) size of an item if the coupon doesn't specify the size, which can sometimes allow couponeers to get items for only pennies or even for free when the coupon is for a fixed amount off.

Couponeers are often stockpilers, since they need to redeem their coupons while they're still valid and a given item is available in the store, regardless of when they intend to use it. Couponeers also tend to buy more prepared foods and cook less from scratch— in contrast to the spontaneous chef—since coupons are less likely to be offered on staples and basic cooking ingredients.

For some people, couponing is more than just about saving money on *their* grocery bill. A number of couponeers told me that instead of giving their children a fixed allowance, they encourage their kids to collect coupons to offset the family grocery bill, with the savings then turned over to the child in cash. Another coupon devotee told me that her favorite wedding gift to give young couples is a zippered coupon organizer stuffed with an assortment of money-saving coupons to help the newlyweds set up housekeeping.

On the other side of the debate are cheapskates like Tim Cuddy. "Ninety-nine percent of coupons are for overpriced, overpackaged, overprocessed crap that you don't need and isn't a good value even with the coupon! Crap is crap, no matter how much you save with a coupon!" No, seriously, Tim, tell me what you think.

Criticisms commonly voiced by the loyal opposition in the great coupon debate include: They take too long to collect and redeem; they're only for brand-name products that still cost more than house brands (even with a coupon); they encourage you to buy things you don't need; they tend to be for processed foods and/or unhealthy foods; and, of course, the risk of paper cuts.

CHEAP SHOT
COUPON MOM

I confess: I'm not a big user of coupons myself (I've never been that organized). But my friend and fellow cheapskate Stephanie Nelson (aka "Coupon Mom") is working hard to make coupons easier to use than ever before. Her website CouponMom.com excites my Inner Miser with the proposition of "cutting your grocery bill in half," and with downloadable coupons and a state-by-state grocery coupon database, she might very well be able to do it. This I know for sure: Unlike some other coupon sites, membership in CouponMom.com is free, and the "Cut Out Hunger" program that Stephanie started on her website lets you help stock your local charitable food pantry with your coupon-clipping activities. Now that *really* excites my Inner Miser.

Savings: Nelson estimates that regular users of her site save **$2,000** per year—and that, she says, is a "conservative" estimate.

Coupon critics are usually highly brand-averse, and cannot be swayed to buy a product because of a brand name. For them, it all comes down to "price per unit." Most supermarkets show the costs of items "per unit" (e.g., by the ounce, pound, count, etc.), along with the total price, on a shelf label where the product is displayed. Because package sizes are often designed to be deceiving—and a coupon may or may not result in a lower price per unit than competing products—you need to always do the math.

As for those cheapskates who only occasionally use coupons, they often tell me that they'll use a coupon only if it's for a product they already plan to buy *and* if it's also on sale. Kind of a belt-and-suspenders approach, I guess.

And the coupon war rages on.

20 Top Grocery Shopping & Cooking Tips from the Cheapskates Next Door

1. **Shop no more than once a week:** Nearly 90 percent of the cheapskates polled go grocery shopping once a week or less often, with some of them shopping as infrequently as once a month. That's a big lifestyle difference: Almost 50 percent of Americans say they shop for groceries *three or four times every week!* Go shopping less, and you'll learn to become a smarter shopper and spend less. It also saves time and gas. It's just that simple.

2. **Ladder your fresh produce:** "But if I shop only once a week, I can't have fresh fruits and vegetables." What a bunch of shiitake! (You know, as in mushrooms.) See Chapter 6 for ideas on storing foods for maximum life expectancy. Learn to "ladder" your fresh produce for the

week. Eat things like bananas and leaf lettuce first—since they can turn quickly—and save the apples and head lettuce for later in the week.

3. **An inconvenient truth:** As comedian Dennis Miller said, "You've got bad eating habits if you use a grocery cart in a 7-Eleven." When you shop at most convenience stores, you're also likely to be spending 50 percent or even more than you'll pay for the same food items on sale at a supermarket. How convenient is that?

4. **Timing is everything:** The cheapskate next door knows that grocery stores and product manufacturers have routine, fairly dependable sale cycles. For example, where we live, if butter is not on sale this week, it most likely will be in the next week or two. It pays to know the cycles and plan accordingly.

5. **Pray for rain:** When stockpiler and Miser Adviser Ralph Huber goes shopping for grocery-store sale items, he's usually hoping they're out of stock. "Since I always shop for things in advance, before I really need them, it's better if something is out of stock and I get a rain check. That way I can pick it up at the sale price whenever I need it."

6. **Make a shopping list based on a menu plan and stick to it:** Sure, you've heard the advice before. But remember that research has shown that approximately 60 percent of all items purchased in grocery stores are "impulse purchases." Be particularly vigilant about avoiding impulse buys on items displayed in the aisles, on aisle "end caps,"

and at the checkout counter—those are traps specifically set by the store to get you to buy something that may not be on your list.

7. **Lunch meat is a bunch of bologna:** Cheapskates like Esther Coyle refuse to pay several dollars per pound for lunch meat at the deli counter. "Cook a chicken, roast a turkey, bake a ham, and make your own lunch meat to freeze," she says. "It tastes so much better and it's healthier, too." Not to mention that it typically costs about 75 percent less than processed lunch meat from the deli counter, based on my shopping experience.

8. **Try it. You'll like it (or not):** Nearly 90 percent of the cheapskates polled said that they at least occasionally buy generic or house-brand items when grocery shopping. Many added that they actually prefer some house brands over some brand-name food products, not just in terms of price, but also for taste/quality. The fact is, the same manufacturer often makes both the brand name and the generic version of a product. It's the same product with different packaging—and price. You owe it to your bank account to at least try less expensive house brands of the products you buy most frequently.

9. **Shopping-cart cheat sheet:** I mentioned earlier that the cheapskate next door has a sixth sense when it comes to knowing how much things should cost and what in fact constitutes a "good deal." And, man, do cheapskates know their grocery prices, continually updating and expanding that databank stored in their frontal lobes. Fellow cheapskates might ask each other "What are you paying for peanut but-

ter?" before they even say hello. If you don't have that sixth sense naturally, make yourself a 3x5 index card listing recent "good prices" for items you buy regularly, and use it to evaluate prices when you go grocery shopping.

10. **Batch it and forget it:** Whether a stockpiler or a spontaneous chef, when we cheapskates cook, we rarely make just a single serving. Batch-cooking is the name of the game. Double, triple, or even quadruple the recipe you're making so you can freeze some for later. Cheapskate John "Doc" Dochnahl of Ennis, Montana, cooks up the makings for his family's favorite burritos—one gallon of pinto beans and two or three elk roasts at a time, freezing pint-sized containers of each for ready access later. (NOTE: Doc also apparently shops at Costco for the twin jumbo-packs of Beano.)

11. **Menu mug shots:** I was surprised by the number of cheapskates who mentioned in passing that they keep a photo album of favorite recipes and meals they've cooked as a reminder and inspiration for future menus. Thanks to them, I've started doing the same, and it really works.

12. **Dollar-store deals:** About three out of four of the cheapskates polled say they "frequently" shop at dollar stores. The biggest dollar-store bargains, they say, include toiletries/ cosmetics, home cleaning products, spices, greeting cards (usually two for a dollar), and snack foods.

13. **BYOB (Be Your Own Butcher):** Learning to cut up a whole chicken, clean your own fish, grind your own hamburger, and otherwise BYOB will save you big money—and

it's kind of fun. Whole chickens at our local supermarket were recently on sale for sixty-nine cents a pound, while a package of "chicken parts" (i.e., a whole chicken cut into parts) sold for $1.49 per pound. With that kind of savings, you get a lot more cluck-for-the-buck if you cut up your own bird.

14. **Don't leave home without it:** Even once you've conditioned yourself to always check the price per unit and put together your shopping-cart cheat sheet, remember that real cheapskates are always armed with a pocket calculator when they go grocery shopping. Particularly if you're using coupons, buying store sale items, or trying to stay within a set budget, doing the math in your head can be difficult, even for a guy like Rob "Rain Man" Crabtree.

15. **"Eat more soup":** One of the touchstone questions I like to ask cheapskates is, "If the economy totally falls apart or you have a personal financial emergency, what would you do?" The answer time and again: "We'd eat more soup!" In good times and bad, we cheapskates love our soup. It's the economical, healthy, easy way to make a meal out of what you have and what you can afford.

16. **A six-and-a-half-pound five-pound bag of apples:** Cheapskate John L. Hoh, Jr., suggests always weighing prepackaged fruits and vegetables, like five-pound bags of apples. "The store has to have a *minimum* of five pounds in each bag," Hoh says. "On occasion, I have found bags with one and a half more pounds than the stated weight . . . and it's the same price as a five-pound bag."

17. **From scratch, but not organic:** Fewer than 5 percent of the cheapskates polled said they buy organic food products, which is on par with the national average. But roughly two-thirds of cheapskates say they cook many foods from scratch (as opposed to buying prepared or processed foods), often citing both health and financial reasons for doing so. Cheapskates apparently aren't convinced that organic is worth the extra cost, but we are committed to eating a healthier diet—particularly when it costs less.

18. **Give yourself a gift of meat on the holidays:** You can always tell who the cheapskates are around most any holiday. We're the ones in the grocery store buying two (or more) hams at Easter, turkeys at Thanksgiving, and corned beefs on St. Patrick's Day. Most supermarkets feature the meat-of-the-season as a deeply discounted loss leader, just to get you to come into the store. At what's usually the lowest price of the year, the cheapskate buys one for now and a couple more to put in the freezer for later.

19. **Meatless Mondays:** Now that you have a freezer full of bargain-priced meat from the holiday sales, consider becoming a vegetarian. Or at least starting a tradition of Meatless Mondays at your house. Fewer than 5 percent of the cheapskates polled said they were vegetarians, which is consistent with the rate of vegetarianism among the general U.S. population. But many cheapskates say they often cook meatless dishes or have a "vegetarian day(s)" at their homes, as a way of both saving money and eating healthier.

20. **The drippins jar:** Having poked around a good many cheapskates' fridges, I'm relieved to know that I'm not the

only one who has a drippins jar. That's what I call the quart jar I keep in our refrigerator. It's the recipient of any and all remnants of salad dressings, jams, jellies, and

---

CHEAP SHOT
BOILED OMELETS FOR A
BARGAIN BRUNCH

When entertaining, brunch is the occasion of choice for many cheapskates. Breakfast foods tend to cost less, with breads and dairy products as the star attractions rather than meats and alcohol, as is often the case with evening affairs. My #1 Fan and Miser Adviser, Wanda Adams of Trotwood, Ohio, turned me on to a fun and frugal way to host a brunch for friends. Give everyone their own quart-size ziplock bag with their name written on it in permanent marker. Guests crack a couple of eggs into their bags, add a dash of milk, and choose their own omelet ingredients from a large selection displayed on a serving tray. The ingredients—bits of meat, shredded cheese, diced veggies—can literally be leftovers from the fridge, tiny portions of each, and the more bizarre the better. Pickled onions, celery tops, or capers, anyone? Seal each bag with no air trapped inside, shake it up good, and drop them all in a large pot of boiling water for fourteen minutes. You'll be amazed at the perfect omelets that emerge, probably costing less than a buck apiece and healthfully prepared without butter or oil.

Savings: I'll bet a boiled omelet brunch for ten will save you **$50–$100** over hosting the same group for a sit-down dinner.

condiments of all kinds. I swish some cider vinegar inside near-empty containers to get out every last drop, and then add it to the drippins jar. This ever-evolving brew makes a great marinade for meat or a delicious salad dressing.

Crock On! It's Not a Cheapskate Kitchen Without One

If cheapskates are a tribe, then the Crock-Pot (aka "slow cooker") is our totem.

Given my own passion for Crock-Pot cooking and the number of slow cookers I saw in use in the kitchens of the cheapskates I visited, I wasn't surprised to find that nearly 95 percent of the cheapskates I polled own at least one, and more than half own at least two. Three cheapskates tied for the top Crock-Pot title, with each claiming to own eight of the appliances! Even the stoic Amish folks I spoke with had a spark of 120-volt envy in their eyes when I mentioned the Crock-Pot, saying with an audible sense of resignation (or so I thought) that they were perfectly content with their stovetop pressure cookers.

Yep, if the status-appliance of the last decade was a $10,000 Viking gas range, then the good old-fashioned Crock-Pot (at about $30 new) is the kitchen appliance du jour for the new economy.

It's little wonder that the cheapskates next door are crazy for their Crock-Pots. Slow cookers are energy-sippers compared to most other cooking methods, even after taking into account the fact that it might take eight hours or even longer to cook a dish in a Crock-Pot. It uses just 100 watts of electricity, which means that if you use it once a week for eight hours at a time, it'll cost you only about thirty cents a *month* in electricity.

Slow cookers can also save you big money when it comes to morphing inexpensive ingredients into mouthwatering meals. The slow cooking process tenderizes inexpensive cuts of meat that might otherwise be tough. Try whole fryers, pork hocks and neck bones, smoked turkey legs and wings, and other inexpensive cuts of beef, pork, lamb, and poultry that you might not otherwise buy. Slow cookers are also great for cooking beans and other legumes, which are among the healthiest—and cheapest—foods you can eat. And because Crock-Pot recipes rarely call for adding extra oil or grease, they're often healthier in that way, too.

Ironically, slow cooking may be even faster than picking up fast food. Most Crock-Pot recipes involve only minutes of prep time, like chopping up a few veggies, stirring together some basic

CHEAP SHOT
UNCORK SOME SAVINGS—
ACCIDENTALWINE.COM

I'm so cheap that I *recant*—as opposed to *de*cant—the wine I serve my dinner guests. In cheapskate vernacular, "recanting" means funneling cheap box-wine into empty premium-label wine bottles to impress wine snobs. No one ever knows the difference. But if you're looking for the real stuff to celebrate a special occasion or give as a gift, check AccidentalWine.com for fine wines at fine prices. The secret to their 20- to 40-percent discounts? As the name implies, they sell quality wines that have been in a little accident . . . like the label on the bottle was damaged in shipping or has been replaced with a new design. Cheers!

Savings: There's a three-bottle minimum order, on which you'll probably save about $20 after shipping costs, depending on your selection.

ingredients, and then turning on the slow cooker and forgetting about it. And while you can cook smaller portions in a slow cooker, most of today's models hold anywhere from four to eight quarts, so they're terrific for batch-cooking, which really saves time and money compared to fast food or dining out. Two favorite slow-cooking-recipe websites of the cheapskate next door are: southernfood.about.com and crockpotrecipes101.com/blog.

Comfort food is a necessity when times are tough. It need not be expensive, and enjoying a simple Crock-Pot meal with friends and family may just remind us of what's really important in life. As my mom always says, "The only thing more important than what's on the table is who's sitting around it."

CHAPTER 12

Don't Laugh. It Gets Me There . . .
and It's Paid For.

**Why is it that people in Hummers and other big-ass SUVs
drive slower than everyone else over those little speed
bumps in parking lots? Isn't this the closest they'll
ever come to an off-road experience?**
—The Ultimate Cheapskate

L et's take my truck."

Pastor Mike Overpeck could see the apprehension on my
face at the prospect of climbing into his 1972 Ford F-100 pickup
truck, a vehicle that looked much older than it truly was, like it
might in fact predate even Mike's boss. (I'm talking about the guy
Mike worked for before he founded the Waterford Community
Church in Goshen, Indiana, not you-know-Who.)

On second thought, Mike's Ford looked like it *could* have been
manufactured BC (Before Chevy).

"Come on! Look who you're riding with. I've got connections,
you know," he said, eyes gazing playfully skyward.

It was a downright cold November morning as we set off
across the ice-glazed roads of northern Indiana, on our way to an
Amish get-together Mike had arranged for me.

He beamed with pride as he told me the history of the truck

and how he'd bought it for only five hundred dollars, with extra emphasis on "I paid cash." Like any cheapskate would be, Mike was clearly proud of the deal he got on his truck and the fact that he relied solely on his own two hands, mechanical know-how, and an occasional prayer to keep it on the road. Hearing him talk about his truck that morning, it struck me that this vehicle had a very special place in Mike Overpeck's wide-open heart.

Mike fiddled with the knobs on the dashboard, and eventually the heater emitted an audible sigh as semi-warm air began wafting from the vents into the cab. For just a moment the windshield clouded as the warm air met the cold glass, and, although I'm not a religious person, I swear that an image of the Virgin Mary appeared plain as day in the condensation on the glass in front of me.

My throat caught for a second. I turned to Mike, who seemed totally oblivious to the religious epiphany I was having in the seat next to him. "Mike, look at that! Does this happen all the time in this truck? Is that who I think it is?" I pointed at the cloudy image on the glass.

"What?" Mike said. "Hey! It looks kind of like Elvis, doesn't it?"

Don't Park Your Stupidity in the Driveway

Mike Overpeck is not alone when it comes to worshipping a good used vehicle, although his faithful Ford is perhaps more divine than most. By more than five to one, the cheapskates next door buy their vehicles used instead of new, another prime example of letting the other guy pay for depreciation. What's more, most of the time they pay cash for those used vehicles, rarely taking out a loan to buy a car.

The cheapskates next door understand something that many

Americans don't: If there's a new car sitting in your driveway, you probably can't afford it. Are you parking your stupidity in the driveway for everyone to see?

"People think that if they can make the monthly car payment, they can afford the car. People also think that having a monthly car payment is a fact of life," Miser Adviser Carl Weiss told me, shaking his head with disbelief. And that's just the mindset car salesmen are hoping that you'll walk into the showroom with, because boy, do they have a deal for you. Carl should know. He sells new cars for a living.

As Carl points out, monthly car payments are just the tip of the dipstick when it comes to the total cost of owning a car, or what is often called the "true cost to own" (TCO). By the time you factor in depreciation, financing, insurance, taxes/fees, fuel, maintenance, repairs, and other costs, the TCO for most cars is usually about twice as much as the purchase price alone (see the TCO calculator at edmunds.com).

But let's just talk about those car payments for a minute and how much car you can really afford. The general rule of thumb is that your car payments should equal less than 15 percent of your take-home pay, and that's assuming that you're not already overly burdened with credit card and other consumer debt—including other car loans.

That means you probably need to be pulling down $80,000 to $90,000 a year (gross) in order to afford a typical new car, costing about $29,000 and financed over four years. According to that guideline, only the top 15 to 20 percent of U.S. households can truly afford to buy a new car. Does that include you?

Of course, most households with that kind of income also have two wage-earners. So make that *two* new cars and $160,000 to $180,000 in income. My Inner Miser is having chest pains.

CHEAP SHOT
SHIFT INTO BIG SAVINGS

As I've told you before, there's nothing shifty about the cheapskates next door. Well, perhaps except for the cars and trucks they drive. Learning to drive a vehicle with a manual transmission can save you serious money. *Consumer Reports* found that cars with manual transmissions get two to four miles per gallon more than the same models with automatic transmissions. But that's only the beginning of the savings. Cars with manual transmissions generally cost less than those with automatic transmissions, and a manual transmission is less expensive to repair or replace when the time comes. Plus, because you're using the car's engine to help you decelerate, manual transmissions are easier on the brakes, saving you even more on maintenance and repairs.

Savings: All told, over the course of your lifetime you'll probably save about 5,000 gallons of gas and **$30,000** or more by driving only cars with manual transmissions.

Stop Huffing the New Car Smell

Apparently that "new car smell"—which is actually a potentially toxic mixture of odors given off by the car's fresh plastic, paint, and upholstery—gets a lot of people stoned out of their minds.

Why else would anyone buy a car that will be worth 20 percent less within the first minute they own it (30 percent less within

the first year), and will likely saddle them with monthly car payments they really can't afford?

The cheapskates next door ain't drinking the Kool-Aid, or
sniffing the glue, as the case may be. They know that there's a
bumper crop of quality used cars on the market today, due in part
to more cars coming on the market through lease programs. Not to
mention all the repos from folks who realized they couldn't in fact
afford a new car once their buzz wore off. Carl Weiss's somewhat
jaded advice for getting a great deal on a virtually new used car?
"Follow the next twenty new car buyers out of my showroom, because at least one in twenty of them is going to default on their car
loan within the first twelve months." Sobering, isn't it?

The cheapskate next door shops for a used car based on the
D4D Principle (Dollars for Durability), and they use *Consumer Reports* for reliability ratings and resale information. They know that
the quality of cars, in general, has steadily increased over the years;
or, as Carl Weiss says, "Nowadays, for most cars, 100,000 miles is
about age forty in car-years," equating the projected life of a car
with the lifespan of a person. But before they lay their money down
for a used car, they usually have a trusted mechanic give it the
once-over and order a vehicle history report from someplace like
carfax.com. Both precautions combined should cost under $100.

What used car should you buy? Cheapskate Gary Price says it's
simple: "Only buy a car you can pay cash for. If you only have
$3,000, then that's all the car you can afford. Buy a late-model used
car and keep it ten to fifteen years if you can." Gary and other
cheapskates start saving for their next car the minute they buy
their current one (see Join the $4 a Gallon Savings Club, on page
183). They let the money in their car-fund earn interest for them,
rather than taking out a car loan and paying interest to a lender.

And finally, maybe you're thinking about leasing a car? Well the cheapskate next door isn't. The conventional wisdom is that leasing *might* make financial sense if you're the kind of person who simply must always drive a new car model, and you've resigned yourself to the fact that you'll always have a monthly car payment to make. Now, *that* doesn't sound like the cheapskate next door, does it?

A Salute to Smart Drivers

I've noticed that people are a lot friendlier on the highways these days, at least around where I live. Every time I go out for a drive, folks always honk and wave at me.

It must be a Maryland thing, though, that unique one-finger wave they use. I always wave back, but since I'm originally from the Midwest, I still use the old-fashioned five-finger wave. It's interesting, because when I smile and wave back, they usually extend their middle finger even more enthusiastically, as they speed around me in the passing lane. It's more like a salute than a wave.

I noticed this change in driver civility on the highways just about the time I declared my own personal War for Energy Independence, after gas prices hit $4 a gallon for the first time ever. That's when I—along with a reported two-thirds of all Americans—started changing my driving habits. The WAD ("Wallet Anxiety Disorder") we were feeling at the pumps made us start to drive smarter, and drive less. And as far as I know, nothing awful happened in our lives because of those changes.

That's when I became über-conscious about consolidating car trips as much as possible, and started depending on my bicycle even more for running errands within a few miles of home. Cheapskate Bruce Jackson calls it his "two-mile challenge," trying to bicycle or walk to any destination within a two-mile radius of his home. That's not only a manageable distance for most people to bike/walk; it's a perfect way to get that thirty to sixty minutes of daily exercise we all need.

Before Clare Thompson puts the key in the ignition, she makes it a point to do the math. She quickly figures out what the trip is

---

CHEAP SHOT
CUT YOUR CHILD MILES

It's no surprise that pretty much every year Americans drive more than they did the year before. But if you dig into the statistics, you'll see that the biggest increase in the miles we drive these days compared to forty years ago isn't in "business commuting miles" (up 36 percent), but in "family and personal business" miles, which have more than tripled: from 1,270 to nearly 4,000 miles per year, according to the National Household Travel Survey. Much of this increase is due to the trend toward chauffeuring our kids to school, their friends' houses, and extracurricular activities. Today an estimated 30 percent of all morning traffic is attributable to parents driving their kids to school, a practice that was virtually unheard of a couple generations ago. It's time to put the kids back on the school bus, have them walk or bicycle to more appointments, and get smart about carpooling with other parents. See walktoschool.org and freerangekids.com for safety tips and ideas.

Savings: Reduce your child miles by even 25 percent, or 1,000 miles, per year, and you could save **$500** or more in annual auto expenses.

going to cost her, based on the federal mileage-reimbursement rate (fifty-five cents per mile in 2009). That's not because she's going to get reimbursed; just the opposite. She's paying for it out of her own pocket. "When I started looking at it that way, it really made me cut down and combine the number of trips I made . . . especially when running errands."

When gas prices hit record highs, that's also when I borrowed a tip from Miser Adviser Brent Cooper and started keeping a glass of water—filled to the brim—in the cup holder in my pickup truck. Within a couple of weeks, this simple trick helped to make me a better, more fuel-efficient driver.

It became a game, as Brent had told me it would, trying to avoid spillage by curbing jackrabbit starts, cornering more carefully, and generally slowing down. I let up on the gas pedal and started sticking to the speed limit, and that's when I noticed that my fellow motorists got a lot friendlier and started waving to me as they passed. Hey buddy, I'll salute you, too, if you *don't* slow down.

Join the $4 a Gallon Savings Club

Despite my reputation as a world-class penny pincher, I'm still paying $4 a gallon for gas. In fact, ever since it hit that record level, I've refused to pay less, even when prices fell by 50 percent or more. I know what you're thinking: "Yeager's lost his money-saving mind! His frugal libido is dead!"

No, you see I've made a pledge to continue to pay $4 a gallon for gas. Or, rather, to pay the lowest price I can find and then bank the difference in my $4 a Gallon Savings Club. It cost about $60 to fill up my Toyota pickup truck when gas was $4 a gallon, and then prices dropped to the point I could fill up for about half that. So,

CHEAP SHOT
WHY OWN A WHOLE CAR?

I have a terrific idea for a new invention: a car with a detachable derriere. I'm thinking a giant zipper, right behind the driver's seat. Why tote along an empty backseat and trunk on trips when you don't need them? Unzip the butt end and leave it parked at home. Until the automotive industry jumps on my idea for zippered cars, Zipcars (ZipCar.com) are the next best thing, particularly if you're an urbanite or live near a college campus. Car-share members pay a nominal annual fee for 24/7 access to a fleet of vehicles parked in lots scattered across their city. Make a reservation by phone or online (last-minute is fine) and use an electronic keycard to access the car. You pay an hourly fee and a per-mile rate, but gas, insurance, maintenance, parking, registration, and taxes—and all the hassles of car ownership—are the company's responsibility. Members spend about $600 per year on car sharing, as opposed to an average of nearly $9,000 annually to own a car, per the AAA.

Savings: Maybe **$8,400** a year if you give up your own car and share one instead.

every time I fill up, I stick what I "save"—the difference between what I would have paid at $4 a gallon, and the price I actually pay—into my Savings Club envelope. Since I fill up about once a week, I squirreled away more than $1,200 over the first twelve months after gas prices dropped below $4 a gallon.

Like the old Christmas Savings Clubs, it's easy to build a nice nest egg by saving a little bit at a time as part of your daily money management routine. Sure, we all complained about paying $4 for a gallon of gas, but we got used to it and adjusted our household budgets and driving behavior to pay for it. And that drop in consumption/demand was one of the primary reasons why gas prices came back down.

Now that the price has dropped, why not bank the savings rather than spend it on something else or, worst of all, go back to our old driving habits? It's a painless way to start building a fund to pay for your next new-used car. After all, I already have enough in my $4 a Gallon Savings Club account to buy two Ford trucks just like Mike Overpeck's miracle mobile.

CHAPTER 13

Cheapskates Come out of the Closet

I buy expensive suits. They just look cheap on me.

—Warren Buffet

Needs: food, clothing, shelter. It doesn't get any more basic than that. Still, I've always thought clothing is a distant third in that classic lineup, if it even belongs in the trifecta at all. And that's not just because of the naturist phase I've been going through lately.

I've never considered clothing a priority, at least when it comes to having a closet packed full of the latest fashions and a selection of shirts, pants, and other apparel in every shade and hue in a Crayola 120-pack. A few basic articles of clothing are all I've ever needed or wanted.

In all honesty, since I left my last full-time job five years ago in order to write, I have spent less than $80 on clothing and never once lacked for something to wear. According to the Bureau of Labor Statistics, that's approximately how much a typical American man my age spends on clothing every *month*. So I've just stretched that monthly budget out a bit; over fifty-nine more months, to be exact.

Clothes seem to last just about forever if you take good care of them. So for an adult, if you keep your tastes—and waistline—

from changing, you're good to go. Or at least that's my approach. Even when I was working in an office, I always lived by Henry David Thoreau's credo: "Beware of all enterprises that require new clothes."

But that's not to say that my extreme austerity when it comes to clothing is for everyone. Personally I'm just disinterested in my appearance in general, and clothing and clothes shopping specifically. That's probably not always a good thing, even for me.

I was reminded of my need for a major fashion makeover during the Florida leg of the Tour de Cheapskate. My book signing in Sarasota, Florida, was scheduled one evening at Sarasota News and Books, a very nice independent bookstore in the upscale part of downtown, just a block off the water. I arrived on my bicycle a little early, after nearly a week and 300 miles of pedaling through days of Florida's famous liquid sunshine, one downpour after the next.

I was dressed as I usually am when cycling, in ratty-looking shorts and a faded T-shirt (GRAND FUNK RAILROAD, as I recall, from the concert I went to in 1978). I decided to take a few moments to relax before the signing, so I sat down on a park bench outside the bookstore with my trusty but tattered ten-speed and well-worn traveling gear parked next to me.

A nicely dressed older woman walked up to me, opened her purse, and tried to hand me a $10 bill, saying, "You poor man, you look like you could use some help." She was there for the signing, and had no idea that I was the author and not a street person . . . although, admittedly, there's often not much difference between the two.

Okay, so maybe it is time for me to rethink my wardrobe and spruce up my appearance a bit. (And, yes, I declined the kind woman's charity, and sold her a couple of copies of my book instead.)

Sensible Fashion Sense

Please don't assume from my own sometimes slovenly appearance that the typical cheapskate next door dresses poorly. Nothing could be further from the truth, despite the fact that they report spending considerably less on clothing than the average American.

In fact, the *Vogue*ishly dressed woman who mistook me for a panhandler in Sarasota turned out to be a world-class cheapskate in her own right and told me she spends less than $100 a year on clothing for herself. I guess my problem is lack of fashion sense, not so much lack of spending.

The average American family of four spends almost $3,000 per year on clothing, although actual spending varies greatly depending on things like the ages and professions of family members. Some of the same variables of course affect how much the cheapskate next door spends on clothing. But on average, of those surveyed, cheapskates usually spend about *one-fourth* as much on clothing as their typical American counterparts. That's right, cheapskates spend about 75 percent less on clothing, but in most cases you'd never know it to look at them.

In short, the cheapskate next door dresses for success, but for much, much less. In fact, almost 30 percent of the cheapskates surveyed said they spend $100 or less on clothing for themselves each year! Their secret lies not only in where and how they shop; it's also in their attitude toward clothing. They buy classic styles instead of trendy ones. They look for quality and durability in clothing, and they're smart enough to know that a famous label or jaw-dropping price tag doesn't necessarily translate into either quality or durability.

Most cheapskates have successfully slain their fashion bug, finding ways to overcome peer pressure and the blitzkrieg of advertising that help make the U.S. fashion industry a nearly $350 billion annual enterprise. Once again, the cheapskate's high degree of self-confidence and self-worth allows her to steer clear of making clothing purchases based on impulse, or on the urge to buy something simply because everyone else is buying one. Because the cheapskate next door is comfortable in her own skin, she's comfortable in whatever clothes appeal to her, regardless of fashion trends and what her friends are wearing.

Miser Adviser Stacie Barnett of Courtland, Illinois, exemplifies cheapskate bravado when it comes to dealing with fashion peer pressure. "It's kind of my *thing* among my group of friends," she told me. "Whenever they start wearing something trendy, I always take a picture so we can all look back and laugh at them, while I'm still looking cool in the same classic stuff I've been wearing for years."

Class Act, Cheapskate Style

Seeking advice on building a classic but affordable wardrobe, I was fortunate to spend some time with "his and her" professional cheapskate designers, if you will. They just happen to live within 150 miles of each other in southern Arizona.

Amy Williams has been an interior designer in Phoenix for twenty-five years, and Bruce Ostyn and Daniel Newman own their own interior design and decorating business in Green Valley, Arizona. All three are proud cheapskates in their personal lives, which proves that high fashion and high prices need not go hand in hand. Given the infamous Sarasota incident, you can imagine my relief in being able to consult with these three style professionals as I sat down to write this chapter.

Amy's advice for the woman's classic closet:

Pick a few colors that look good on you and together, and then build your wardrobe so everything can
be worn with everything else. For interest, add a cheap
piece with some fun color. For example, I use inexpensive fun-color tank tops ($5 new) under dark classic-
style V-necks over pants or a skirt, which is much more
versatile than a dress. If I am going to work, I can throw
a blazer and some funky costume jewelry on to dress it
up to "designer" standards. Layer—it keeps you warm
and you can wear basic casual wear and dress it up for
the office.

Buy quality on sale. Buy classic colors and styles, except for some fun accent pieces. Add accessories, not more
clothes. Buy mostly cheap earrings and necklaces with
color to mix/match. Buy only what you *love*, otherwise
you will be trading it yearly instead of keeping it until
you've worn it out. If you can find classic designer brands
at the resale store or at a great sale price, that is your
best bet.

Daniel and Bruce offer similar suggestions for the cheap gen-
tleman's wardrobe, focusing on a few basic colors and classic styles
that work for you, and then choosing shirts and other items that
can be incorporated into multiple outfits. Again, the emphasis is on
avoiding trendy styles that will quickly become outdated, and creating diversity in your wardrobe by choosing items that can be
worn in various combinations, rather than simply buying more
clothes.

I was particularly heartened to hear Bruce and Daniel's views
on fashion in general. Here are two style professionals who aren't
afraid to tell the Emperor what they think of his new set of clothes:

Ignore advertising, buy quality, and don't be afraid to wear the hell out of it. Whatever we wear is fashionable. It may be our fashion, but who wants to be a trend follower? Our taste is for us and no one else. We don't have the time or inclination to try to look like what manufacturers tell us we should look like. Though we do buy quality clothing when we buy it, and then we wear it until it wears out.

As for my GRAND FUNK RAILROAD T-shirt? All three of my cheapskate fashion consultants politely declined to comment.

CHEAP SHOT
HOST A NAKED LADY PARTY
(AND BE SURE TO INVITE ME)

Miser Adviser Julie Hall immediately aroused my frugal libido when she told me about the "Naked Lady Parties" she's fond of having with her budget-conscious girlfriends. The group of similar-sized young ladies meets a couple of times a year to strip down and swap items from their clothes closets that they're bored with. It's usually a dinner affair, potluck of course, and they take turns hosting it at each other's homes. I issued a standing invitation to host it at my place, but so far I'm still waiting.

Savings: Variable, but the average single woman in the United States spends about $1,100 on clothing every year, so reduce that by just 10 or 20 percent by hosting a Naked Lady Party and you'll save $110–$220.

Where, When, and How Cheapskates Shop for Clothes

Of course there's some diversity of opinion among cheapskates when it comes to shopping for clothes, but here are some clothes shopping fundamentals from the questionnaire:

"Resale stores are the bomb!"—Amy Williams

Most of those surveyed reported buying a majority of their clothes secondhand instead of new, with consignment or resale shops generally preferred over thrift stores for clothes shopping. Shopping at thrift stores in upscale neighborhoods was frequently mentioned as well. Yard and rummage sales were not as popular for clothes shopping, due to their uncertain selection and the amount of time required to locate and shop at them.

"We seldom buy anything new unless it's at least 75 percent off."—Daniel Newman

When cheapskates do buy new clothing, they virtually never pay full price, waiting until they find what they're looking for on sale. Retail clothing stores favored by the cheapskates next door run the gamut from "the marts" (Walmart, Kmart, Target, etc.) to the bargain racks at upscale stores like Neiman Marcus. Conspicuously absent from the list are trendier national chains like Old Navy, Banana Republic, and the Gap, although more cost-conscious national and regional chains like T.J. Maxx, Marshalls, and Burlington Coat Factory are cheapskate favorites for clothes shopping.

"I think Bush was still president. And I'm talking about the first Bush."—Cheapskate Tom Dempsey, talking about the last time he went clothes shopping

Not surprisingly, the cheapskate shops for clothes relatively infrequently, usually no more than twice a year. The exception is cheapskates who have young children (see Chapter 4), in which case they usually shop for children's clothing on an ongoing basis throughout the year, both to take advantage of end-of-season sales and keep pace with their growing progeny. For cheapskate families with young children, thrift stores, resale shops, and occasional yard sales are most popular, given that children usually outgrow their clothes before they wear them out, and, as more than one cheapskate told me, "a two-year-old doesn't know that he's wearing secondhand clothes."

**"Keep a continuous list of clothes you need to buy. NEVER buy anything if it's not on the list . . . and then only if it's on sale."
—Miser Adviser Betty Jacob**

Once again, organization and premeditated shopping saves the cheapskate mucho dinero.

"I know if I look good in it in the middle of winter, I'll look even better in it next summer."—Cheapskate Helen Butler, talking about another benefit (besides discount prices) of buying swimwear out of season

Helen is a proud member of a cheapskate sect I call the "Discount Druids," cheapskates who specialize in off-season bargains. Like Helen, Discount Druids can often be found trying on half-priced Speedos at the Sports

Authority while most shoppers are trying on ski boots and parkas.

My Underwear Could Qualify as a National Historic Site

Knowing where, when, and how to shop for clothing is important—as is slaying your fashion bug and not getting caught up in trendy styles—but when it comes to the drawers-dropping pittance that most cheapskates spend on clothing compared to other folks, they have one other secret hiding in their closet. You might say *time is on their side.*

CHEAP SHOT
DRYER LINT: WORTH MORE THAN GOLD?

I like to think of dryer lint as spendthrift's gold. While an ounce of dryer lint might not be worth more than an ounce of gold, it represents the life of your expensive clothes being cooked and beaten out of them by an electric or gas dryer. Drying clothes in a dryer—as opposed to on a clothesline—can cut the lifespan of some clothing by as much as half. Most people don't calculate the amortized cost of their underwear based on the life expectancy of their briefs, but when you do the math, the savings to be had by using the old-fashioned clothesline can be considerable. Plus electric/gas dryers cost about $110 per year on average to own and operate.

Savings: Use a clothesline to extend the life of your clothing by even 10 percent, and an average family of four will save about $400 per year, including the annual savings on the dryer.

A full 90 percent of the cheapskates polled say that they wear their clothes until they're totally worn out and ready for the rag bag. Ironically but sadly, roughly 90 percent of all clothing thrown away in the United States is *not* "worn out," meaning threadbare, torn, or horribly stained. Apparently, other than the noble cheapskate, most Americans have little shame about tossing out perfectly wearable clothes.

Bruce and Daniel spoke for most cheapskates when they told me, "We wear *all* of our clothes until they're worn out. Then they turn into clothes to wear when we work in the yard, and then they turn into clothes that we wear while painting, and then finally we cut them up and use them as rags. It's like losing a friend when we consign a shirt to the rag bin."

Most cheapskates say they expect new clothing—which of course they rarely buy—to last at least seven to ten years, not including clothes that their kids outgrow. Popular cheapskate tips for getting the most life out of clothing include: Wash clothes in cold water only; launder less frequently; dry clothes on a clothesline (see Cheap Shot), and keep a written inventory of the clothes you have in storage so that you remember to wear them. Off-season clothes should be stored in plastic totes (preferably not clear-sided) with a couple of cedar blocks placed inside for extra protection.

Perhaps contrary to public perception, very few cheapskates (less than 5 percent) report making their own clothes on a regular basis. But "clothes remodeling," as Miser Adviser Evelyn Edgett calls it, is quite popular among the cheap set. Dresses are transformed into blouses, long pants with worn-out knees are amputated to wear as summer shorts, and a tired trousseau is updated and customized to look new again. Evelyn recommends the book *Sew Subversive* (Taunton, 2006) for anyone interested in refashioning instead of replacing their wardrobe.

And last, but perhaps most admirably, more than 80 percent

of the cheapskates surveyed report currently owning a garment that's twenty years old or older, and that they still wear at least occasionally.

Of course those are still new threads for a guy like Bruce Jackson. Bruce took top prize in the Old Duds Division, still proudly sporting a Woolrich jacket his father bought in 1938. FDR was president back then, and I think he famously said something like: "We have nothing to fear but fashion itself."

CHEAP SHOT
DON'T GET TAKEN TO THE DRY CLEANERS

Dry cleaning is a $9 billion a year business in the United States, and with all the chemicals it involves, it's one that's notoriously hard on the environment. Go green—and keep more green in your wallet—by avoiding DRY-CLEAN ONLY clothing and using less expensive, less toxic cleaning methods for some dry-cleanable items. According to an article in *Consumer Reports* (ConsumerReports.org), "Dry-cleaning isn't the only way to safely clean garments labeled dry-clean only, and other methods might even do a better job." Hand-washing items in cold water and air drying them is an acceptable alternative to dry cleaning in many instances. Even jackets and other structured garments that have a lining and should be dry cleaned can often be dry-cleaned at home using inexpensive products like Dryel and Dry Cleaner's Secret.

Savings: Variable, but households that regularly take clothes to the dry cleaner can likely save at least $100 a year by cutting back on or eliminating the process entirely.

CHAPTER 14

Insurance: Betting on Yourself

I don't want to tell you how much insurance I carry with the Prudential, but all I can say is: When I go, they go, too.
—Jack Benny

A bishop and two Amish appraisers go to a farm to see a cow that was struck by lightning." Sounds like the first line of a corny joke, doesn't it?

No, it's Levi's attempt to explain to me the Amish method of self-insurance, or "free-will offerings." I'm seated at an eighteen-foot-long dining room table—rather, a choo-choo train of smaller tables strung together—under the soft bluish glow given off by overhead propane lighting fixtures.

Levi's extended family is in attendance, including his parents, all his children and their spouses, and a burgeoning crop of grandchildren. I'm chaperoned by Mike Overpeck and his family, who arranged for me to have dinner at Levi's house outside of Goshen, Indiana.

We've just finished a massive Amish dinner prepared by Levi's wife and daughters, a gastronomical gorge-fest that has me seriously considering relinquishing my "English" ways and becoming Amish on the spot. Any religion that serves five kinds of dessert has my vote, and that was before I knew that the deal included property and health insurance. Plus, think of the savings on shaving supplies.

I wrote in my first book about my fascination, bordering on obsession, with the Amish and their simpler way of life. Sure, part of that is the result of follicle envy, the jealousy I've always felt toward guys who can effortlessly grow robust quantities of facial hair, in contrast to my own mangy-dog attempts at growing a beard in the past. (Oh, for even one Yeager family gathering where we don't need to recall those stories and pull out the snapshots.)

But mostly I respect the Amish because they carefully consider the question of whether change is always progress, and whether progress is in all ways positive. No, I'm not advocating that we all give up electricity, automobiles, and our Gillette Trac IIs to become Amish, but the fact that the Amish don't always allow the changing world around them to change their lives seems like a concept the rest of us might benefit from considering from time to time.

While I'd known something about the Amish stand on technology from the research I did for my first book, my dinner with Levi and his family was a real eye-opener regarding many other admirable aspects of Amish life. At first I thought Levi was yanking my English chain about "Amish appraisers" and cows getting struck by lightning. That was a distinct possibility, given the keen wit and love of laughter I'd discovered—much to my surprise and delight—among nearly all of the Amish folks I met. Yet Another Amish Ambush.

In fact, Levi was being absolutely serious. Amish communities across the country contribute funds through their local parishes to, in essence, self-insure against both property and medical losses. It's sort of an extension of the idea of Amish barn raising, the collective effort of the community to sustain itself with minimal help from outside.

This free-will system is much more complicated and codified than I'd ever imagined, involving designated Amish appraisers and annual reporting of assets and other property. If a family or community suffers a catastrophic loss, as Amish in the Goshen area did a few years ago when a tornado struck, free-will funds (and extra pairs of helping hands) are tapped from Amish communities across the country. It's a self-sustaining system that has served the Amish for ages.

Given the unraveling of the U.S. insurance industry that was underway as I sat in Levi's dining room helping myself to a third piece of custard pie, I couldn't help but think that if AIG stood for "Amish Insurance Group," we'd likely not be in the mess that we're in.

And, yes, apparently cows do get struck by lightning on a fairly regular basis, at least in the Land of Goshen. Who knew?

Controlling Insurance Costs by Controlling Your Life

While the cheapskates next door rarely self-insure to the extent the Amish do, they definitely lean toward betting on themselves when it comes to buying insurance.

They frequently take out policies with large deductibles, having amassed sufficient savings to make that a smart move. They understand that insurance costs—both in terms of premiums and which types of insurance you need to carry—are impacted by some things that you can at least partially control, including:

- what you own
- how you live
- where you live
- your health
- how much debt, savings, and other assets you have

"Most people never stop and think about the fact that if you own a more modest home and less stuff—as well as less expensive stuff—you'll save big money on insuring everything. It really adds up over the years," says cheapskate Barb Sanderson, commenting on an often unappreciated benefit of living more simply.

Because cheapskates frequently buy used items, live in less expensive homes, and drive their cars until they're no longer roadworthy, the value of what they need to insure is less—and so, too, are the premiums they pay. Using auto insurance as an example, it usually makes sense to drop collision and comprehensive coverage entirely if you're paying an annual premium that is 10 percent or more of the value of your car. So, if your car is worth only $2,000 and you're paying more than $200 annually for collision and comprehensive, you might want to consider dropping collision and comprehensive coverage and saving those premiums.

Another cheapskate strategy for reducing insurance costs is to take on more of the risk yourself by purchasing home, auto, and health insurance (see below) with higher deductibles. This makes sense if you've been living below your means and thus have built a sufficient cushion of savings. Higher deductibles on car insurance can save you up to 30 percent in premiums, and increasing your home insurance deductible to, say, $5,000 from $250 could save you even more than 30 percent. Bank what you save on premiums in a sinking fund (see Chapter 3) to pay possible out-of-pocket deductible amounts.

When it comes to life insurance, the cheapskate once again has an advantage. If you're debt-free and accustomed to living on a modest amount of money, your perspective on the amount of life insurance you need to carry—and perhaps whether you need to carry any at all—may very well change. Life insurance is usually purchased to mitigate the loss of a wage earner's income in the event of his/her death, and to make sure survivors can continue to meet their mortgage payments, the kid's college tuition, and other obligations.

The general rule of thumb when buying life insurance is to buy a policy equal to five to ten times your annual gross income. But if you're accustomed to spending considerably less than your current income and you're debt-free, those factors need to be part of the equation. That said, parents with dependent children almost always need to have life insurance, and rates for term life insurance, which is usually the best choice, have become increasingly afford-able (see Cheap Shot).

CHEAP SHOT
LIFE KEEPS GETTING CHEAPER

"I'm not only getting cheaper every year, but my life insurance seems to be doing the same," cheapskate Mark Baxter told me. If you've had a term life insurance policy in effect for even a few years, you might be in for a very pleasant surprise should you take the time to shop around for coverage: Term life insurance rates have dropped by about half since the mid-1990s. Ask your current insurer if new lower rates might apply, and then shop the competition online at the sites Term4Sale.com and Insure.com. If you decide to switch policies, the most important thing to remember is to get the new policy in place before you cancel your current one. That way, if you fail the medical exam or some other glitch comes up, you won't be left without coverage.

Savings: Will vary depending on your age, lifestyle, location, etc., but Mark Baxter lowered his annual premiums by about $250 a year.

Knowledge Is Key . . . and It's Free!

Once again, the cheapskates next door know what they want to buy and what they want to pay when they go shopping for insurance.

"Insurance is another example of something most people buy, and then never bother to review or shop around again," says Barb Sanderson. She and other cheapskates advocate getting at least two other price quotes for comparison purposes whenever your insurance policies come up for renewal. Also call your current agent whenever a policy is up for renewal, and ask about ways to reduce costs.

It's easy to get comparison quotes on websites like Insurance .com, NetQuote.com, and InsWeb.com. Choose a highly rated insurance company (see ambest.com for ratings), but don't pay more out of *company loyalty*; it isn't worth it. If given a reason to raise your rates, do you think your insurance company won't do so out of a sense of *customer loyalty?*

A majority of the cheapskates surveyed reported that they "bundle" their auto and homeowner's insurance (and sometimes other policies) into a package policy with a single insurance company. This practice frequently lowers total premiums 10 percent or even more, although I still advise shopping each component policy around separately as well, just to be safe. A number of cheapskates also take advantage of lower-priced insurance programs and discounts available through their college alumni associations and other professional organizations.

And finally, it's important to really understand the coverage you're paying for, both to take full advantage of the benefits and to eliminate unnecessary and duplicative coverage in the future. Cheapskate Julie Hall was thrilled to discover that her health insurance would pick up the tab for the Weight Watchers program she was enrolled in, and Julia Thomson shaved $400 off her auto insurance premium by doing the math and figuring out that rental car coverage, windshield damage protection, and collision coverage on her aged car wasn't worth the extra cost. Also, if you're a member of AAA you probably don't need towing coverage under your auto insurance policy.

One more time: *The most important economy is the one I create myself.*

CHEAP SHOT
CHEAP MEDS, HOLD THE MEMBERSHIP

Looking for inexpensive prescription drugs? You may have heard that most of the major membership warehouse stores, including Costco, Sam's Club, and BJ's Wholesale Club, now have pharmacies on premises and online. They're filling prescriptions at truly bargain prices—like 20 to 50 percent less than many other pharmacies, with even bigger savings on generics. But what you may not have heard is that since pharmaceuticals are regulated by the federal government, membership warehouse clubs can't require you to be a member in order to buy prescription drugs there (nor to purchase eyeglasses or booze!). Miser Adviser John Hoh, Jr., alerted me to this membership loophole, but cautions that the people checking membership cards at the door may not be aware of it, so you may need to ask for the manager to gain entrance.

Savings: The average American over the age of thirty-five pays more than $500 annually for prescription drugs, so the savings could be **$125–$250** or more.

Health Insurance: Don't Go Bare, but Maybe Go Topless

As my favorite living philosopher, Kinky Friedman, is fond of saying, "I'm too young for Medicare and too old for women to care."
That pretty much sums up my situation. And I'm not alone, at least
when it comes to securing affordable health insurance prior to
being eligible for Medicare (typically at age 65—see medicare.gov).

Roughly 75 percent of health insurance carried by Americans
is through employer-provided programs, and that percentage is
dropping as more and more employers discontinue medical benefits for their employees. If you're in that 75 percent, go to work
every day and thank your employer. At the same time, many employers are also scaling back on the portion of health care costs
they'll pick up, leaving employees to shoulder more of the costs
themselves.

Then there are the rest of us—those without access to health
care through our employers, and still too young for Medicare.
Forty-five million Americans simply go without health insurance,
unable to afford it. The rest of us bend over and cough, doing whatever it takes to secure some level of health care protection in the
only industrialized nation in the world without a universal health
insurance system. I'm speaking of course of the U.S.A., or at least
the non-Amish part of the U.S.A. (Ironic, isn't it? You might consider the Amish to be a nonindustrialized nation within an industrialized nation, yet arguably they have universal health care while
the rest of us don't. Go figure.)

Given the proclivity of cheapskates next door for being *self-*
ishly employed—working for themselves or in careers chosen more
out of passion than salary or benefit considerations—it's little
wonder that a greater percentage of cheapskates find themselves in
the position of securing health insurance on their own. Almost 40

percent of those surveyed said that they purchase health insurance on their own, without the benefit of an employer-provided plan. That's not to suggest that cheapskates have a solution to America's health care crisis, but most of us do have an Amish-esque approach to the problem.

"We call it *house insurance*, not *medical insurance*," Jacquie Phelan told me. "If we didn't own a house that we could lose if we get sick or have an accident, we'd probably go bare . . . We wouldn't carry any medical insurance, and would risk bankruptcy." A copy of the infamous calendar featuring Jacquie clad only in mud is sitting on the table next to us as we talk. Even though I knew what she meant by "go bare," my eyes involuntarily flash to the calendar on the table, and I blush when she catches me.

Jacquie and her husband, Charlie, tackle the health insurance dilemma the same way Denise and I do, along with most of the other cheapskates I spoke to who lack access to employer-provided health care. We don't go bare, but we do *go topless*.

Particularly if you're in relatively good health, it often makes sense to purchase a health insurance plan with a very large annual deductible (like $5,000—$10,000), but much lower monthly premiums. Under these so-called "High Deductible Health Plans," or HDHP (see allhealth.org), you cover the up-front deductible amounts out of your own pocket—that's why I call it *going topless*—and the insurance kicks in once the deductible is met. And qualified HDHPs sometimes cover 100 percent of expenses after the deductible is met, making them potentially superior to traditional health plans in catastrophic situations, in terms of maximum out-of-pocket expense liability.

It's pretty easy to do the math on various insurance plans and figure out where your particular break-even point is when it comes to taking on a larger deductible. But if you decide on an HDHP, the

CHEAP SHOT
STAVING OFF DEATH AND TAXES

I know, the only two things in life you can't avoid: death and taxes. But if your employer offers a Flexible Savings Account (FSA) program, it can at least help you a little bit on both fronts. FSAs allow you to avoid payroll taxes (federal and state taxes, as well as FICA) on a portion of your earnings that you set aside to pay for qualified medical expenses, and often for dependent care and other expenses. If your employer offers an FSA program and you have qualifying medical or other expenses, you're probably losing out on serious savings if you don't participate. Taxes and FICA can easily eat up forty cents of every dollar you earn, so if you set aside, say, $1,000 in an FSA, you'll save about $400. You can't use the funds in your FSA to pay for health insurance premiums, but rather for medical expenses not paid for by insurance—including, typically, deductibles, copayments, coinsurance, over-the-counter drugs, etc. You must use up funds deposited in your FSA annually, or you'll lose what's left. The key to avoiding any forfeiture is to budget carefully, based on the actual amount you spent in the prior year, plus/minus any major changes in medical or other qualified expenses you foresee in the upcoming year. See IRS Publication 502 for details.

Savings: Variable, but **$400** a year in the above example.

important thing is to put what you save on premiums into a sinking fund to pay possible out-of-pocket expenses. In most situations it's possible to set up a Health Savings Account, or HSA (see IRS Publication 969), in which to deposit these funds on a tax-advantaged basis. HSAs have some of the same advantages as Flexible Spending Accounts (see Cheap Shot), but can be set up by self-employed individuals and don't have the "use it or lose it" feature of an FSA.

CHAPTER 15

Cheapskates Just Wanna Have Fun

**The U.S. Constitution doesn't guarantee happiness,
only the pursuit of it. You have to catch up with it yourself.**
—Benjamin Franklin

As I mentioned earlier, it will come as no surprise to my publisher that if you're looking for the cheapskate next door during his free time, you're likely to find him at the public library. A full 90 percent of those cheapskates surveyed said they frequently visit their local library, almost twice the national average reported by the American Library Association.

While sales of my first book have been steady enough, I hear from a great many fans of the book who admit—sometimes sheepishly, but more often proudly—that they of course borrowed it from their local library rather than purchased a copy of their own. I say *Bravo!*, since I'm a big supporter of America's public library system. But I've seen my publisher grimace on occasion at the thought of all the individual-copy sales they might otherwise be racking up if it weren't for cheapskates lovin' their public libraries so much.

In fact, a few months after the book was released, I had a dream that my editor called me and said she had both good news and bad news about the market response to my book. "The good news is," she said in my dream, "more than a million people have already read your book. The bad news is, we've sold only twenty-seven copies."

But of course libraries buy the copies they loan out, so everybody wins. And I've been flattered to hear from many libraries across the country that my little book is one of their most popular nonfiction requests. At the same time, I've heard from a good many cheapskates who have written to say they enjoyed my book so much that they spent every lunch hour for the past two weeks standing in the back of Barnes & Noble to read the whole thing. These are inevitably the fan letters that end with "P.S.—Can't wait to read your next book!" Yet again, *c'est la cheapskate.*

Free Time That's Truly Free (or At Least Cheap)

The cheapskates next door love their leisure time just like everybody else. But, as you might guess, we don't necessarily think you need to spend a lot of money to enjoy yourself or have fun.

In response to the question "If you had the option, would you decrease your working hours and wages to increase your leisure time?," roughly seven out of ten cheapskates said they would, and almost 20 percent indicated that at some point in their lives they did just that. As discussed earlier, cheapskates tend to place a premium on "having experiences" as opposed to "having stuff," so free time for leisure, recreation, and spending with family and friends is a prized commodity for the cheapskate next door.

Here's how we get the most out of our free time, while spending the least:

- **We make our own fun.** In general, we don't like to pay other people to entertain us or enjoy activities that involve a lot of (expensive) equipment. "It's my $2 Xbox," Stan Chesler said,

CHEAP SHOT
VOLUNTEER FOR ALL THE FUN

As I mentioned before, the cheapskates next door give generously of both their money and their time to a wide range of nonprofit, church, and other civic organizations. But part of the reason many of them like to volunteer is because it can be a lot of free fun. Rita Rush, for example, is a volunteer usher at her local community theater in the Chicago area, which means she gets to see all of the shows for free. Volunteering is its own reward, but as Rita knows, sometimes it comes with some pretty nice fringe benefits too. Fun and rewarding volunteer opportunities are as wide-ranging as volunteer organizations themselves, from helping with the annual Audubon Society Christmas bird count to being a Civil War reenactor at Gettysburg Battlefield to learning a foreign language by tutoring someone in English. Check out these websites for volunteer opportunities in your area: VolunteerMatch .org, Idealist.org, BeTheChange.org.

Savings: Variable, but in Rita's case, by being a volunteer usher she saves herself **$300** for a season ticket pass; plus she knows every song in *The Music Man* by heart.

referring to the pack of playing cards he carries with him at all times (even to church). Playing cards and board games, doing puzzles, reading, and simply talking with family and friends are top cheapskate forms of indoor entertainment.

• **We're participants more than spectators.** Fewer than 10 percent of the cheapskates polled said that they attend profes-

sional sporting events, but playing sports like softball, basket-
ball, football, badminton, and hockey—as well as attending
public school sporting events (usually free!)—were all mentioned as popular cheapskate activities.

- **We often enjoy pastimes that save us or make us money.**
"It's not work if you enjoy it," Bob Ferris told me about his
passion for home remodeling. He's remodeled his entire house
himself—three different times. Money-saving activities like
home remodeling, gardening, cooking, sewing, and car repair
are popular leisure-time activities for many cheapskates, and
some have actually turned their skills into cottage industries
in their spare time.

- **We get the most out of our public institutions.** It's not just
public libraries that catch the cheapskate's fancy, it's public
institutions of all kinds, including museums, parks, civic organizations, schools, churches, colleges, and universities. The cheapskates get involved, often as volunteers (see Cheap Shot),
because they know that public institutions and organizations
provide a broad range of activities, events, and services at little
or no charge. "In our retirement, having a university nearby
with all the free lectures and concerts and other events has been
wonderful," said cheapskate Joyce Yeager (aka "The Mother of
All Cheapskates").

- **We like being outside.** Favorite cheapskate recreational and
leisure-time activities often involve the great outdoors—in
part, I suspect, because Mother Nature usually gives herself
away for free. Walking, hiking, camping, running, bicycling,
bird-watching, rock collecting, canoeing, and fishing were all
indicated as favorite outdoor activities enjoyed by the cheapskates next door.

- **We like the arts (and the crafts).** Singing, playing musical
instruments, and performing onstage were surprisingly com-

CHEAP SHOT
NUTTY FOR NETFLIX

I always try to shy away from any type of blatant product endorsement, and I don't accept any commercial advertisements on my website or have any corporate sponsors. (Of course, I can't imagine what company would want America's cheapest man as their official spokesmiser.) That said, I'm struck by the number of cheapskates I've met who share my love for Netflix, the online DVD rental outfit, so I feel a plug is in order. Sure, you can borrow DVDs from the library, but their selection is often limited, you need to go there to pick them up and return them, and some libraries even charge for DVD rentals. With Netflix, you pay a flat monthly fee (our plan costs $16.99 a month), and you select from over 100,000 DVD titles on their website. The DVDs you request are mailed to you and usually arrive in a single day—amazing service. You can keep them as long as you like (no late fees), and rent as many as you want in a month, just so long as you don't have more than three checked out at any one time. To return them, they give you a nifty, postage-paid return envelope that you just drop in the mail.

Savings: Compared with conventional DVD rental stores, if you rent three movies a week you'll probably save more than $500 a year by joining Netflix— and that doesn't include the cost of late fees, membership fees, and the gas you'll burn up with most rental stores.

mon interests among the cheapskates polled, as were painting, drawing, and writing poetry. Often more "crafty" hobbies— like scrapbooking, jewelry making, knitting, and candle making—were mentioned as enjoyable pastimes and also as ways to make affordable gifts for friends and family.

- **And, yes, we have some weird hobbies.** Some strange but true pastimes enjoyed by the cheapskates next door ("So *that's* what they're doing over there!"): moss gardening, making paper from dryer lint, creating dolls out of vegetables, collecting twisty seals, soap carving, making modern art sculptures from computer heat-sinks salvaged from the landfill, weaving with pet hair, building miniature models of Biblical events inside Corona beer bottles, knitting with plastic grocery bags, playing the glass harmonica, and, of course, collecting road kill (for taxidermy, or sometimes just for fun).

On the Road with the Cheapskate Next Door

It would be a mistake to assume that all cheapskates are homebodies, cloistered in their humble abodes for fear that if they venture out into the world it would cause their Spending Anxiety Disorder to flare up.

Just like everybody else, some cheapskates prefer to spend their leisure and vacation time around home, but a good many like to hit the road and see the world. In response to the question "When it comes to leisure time, would you generally rather spend that time *at home* or *away from home* doing something?," the most common response was something along the lines of "Some of both," followed by "Away from home," and finally "At home."

When it comes to travel, the cheapskates next door have a fairly high level of interest and consider it relatively important, despite the expense. In response to the question "On a scale of one to ten, with one being *no interest whatsoever* and ten being *an extraordinary level of interest,* how interesting/important is traveling to you?," responses averaged out to about a seven and a half.

Is the average cheapskate more cosmopolitan than the typical American? It surprised me to discover that more than two-thirds of the cheapskates polled said that they have traveled outside the United States at least once in their lifetime. That's quite high, given that fewer than 25 percent of Americans own passports.

So how do the cheapskates next door manage to take vacations, and in some cases travel the globe, without giving their Inner Misers an incurable case of stress-induced Montezuma's revenge? There is no one model for vacationing/traveling cheapskate style. A lot depends on your family situation and what you consider to be a "vacation."

Daniel Newman and Bruce Ostyn are what you might call *cheapskate vagabond travelers.* They prefer independent travel over group or "package" tours, and believe that by living like the locals do when they travel, the value of the travel experience is enhanced. And it also costs a lot less.

The selfishly employed couple travels at least eight to twelve weeks out of the year just for fun, mostly sleeping in the very comfortable camper kit they bought for their pickup truck and cooking many of their own meals. "I love to cook," Daniel says, "so part of the travel adventure for us is shopping in different local markets and trying new ingredients we don't cook with at home." They do bring some basic food supplies with them from home, like ramen noodles (you remember, the ones they keep in the dishwasher).

I would estimate that about half of the avid cheapskate travelers I've met fit the vagabond traveler profile. They camp, stay with friends or family, or even stay at youth hostels (see Cheap Shot, page 218) or CouchSurf (see Cheap Shot, page 127) when they travel.

They usually cook most or all of their own meals themselves when traveling, and they typically enjoy outdoor activities like hiking, bicycling, and bird-watching (a favorite for Bruce and Daniel), which are commonly free or inexpensive.

They often travel for longer periods of time, more in the European "holiday" tradition. Europeans typically have two or three times (or even more) the amount of vacation per year than most Americans, yet on average they spend about the same amount of money as Americans spend for their much shorter vacations. We Americans apparently feel a greater urge-to-splurge during our vacations, perhaps because they're so short.

There is another distinct type of cheapskate traveler, one who enjoys more traditional, perhaps less adventuresome vacations, but who rarely pays full price. You might call such folks the *value vigilante vacationers*, because they take matters into their own hands when it comes to finding rock-bottom prices on vacation travel. They prefer five-star hotels to sleeping under the stars; they prefer to eat their meals at restaurants rather than roadside rest areas; and they prefer tour guides and concierge service to guidebooks and help-yourself service. But value vigilante vacationers also prefer to pay less than full freight.

Here are some tips from the value vigilante vacationers I polled:

• These cheapskates manage to pay for most or even all of a vacation with mileage points, cash-back, or other travel awards they earn throughout the year by using their credits cards to pay for virtually everything they buy. Of course, they then pay off the entire balance every month (see Chapter 3). Those who travel on business also maximize frequent flyer points on airlines, and frequent guest points at the hotels they stay at, so they can redeem them when the family vacation rolls around (if their employer's travel policy allows). Compare different credit

card travel rewards and other benefit programs at CreditCards
.com/reward.php, and see SmartTraveler.com for information
on selecting the best frequent flyer program for you.

- *When* you travel is undoubtedly the biggest factor influencing
  how much you'll pay. Off-season travel is usually when you'll
  find the best bargains (and smallest crowds). But if you're
  not able to travel off-season, even a day or two difference can
  save you mucho dinero on airfares, hotels, rental cars, and
  travel packages. See the websites AirFareWatchDog.com and
  FareCompare.com to figure out the cheapest days/times to fly,
  and use SideStep.com to comparison shop for the best deals on
  flights, hotels, rental cars, and cruises, all compiled from over
  two hundred other websites.

- Contact the chambers of commerce and tourist information
  bureaus for the areas you'll be visiting before you leave home
  and ask them to send you a complete info packet. These usually contain discount coupons and special offers from local hotels, restaurants, and other attractions.

- If you're traveling by car on your vacation, consider renting
  one rather than driving your own. Since most rental cars now
  come with unlimited mileage, you may be better off renting a
  car if you plan on driving a lot of miles in a relatively short period of time, particularly if the rental gets better gas mileage
  than your own car. Plus, if you have a breakdown on the road,
  you won't lose a day or two of your vacation waiting for your
  car to get repaired, since most major rental companies can
  supply a replacement vehicle pronto. Check websites like
  Expedia.com and CarrentalExpress.com for the best deals on
  rental cars.

- Buy an Entertainment Book (entertainment.com) for the
  area(s) you'll be visiting for savings on travel, dining, and spe-

cial attractions. See Chapter 8 for other savings tips on restaurant meals when you're traveling, including discount-meal gift certificates from Restaurant.com.

- Bring the ingredients for your favorite cocktails, or other alcoholic beverages, from home to avoid the high cost of buying alcoholic drinks in restaurants and bars. Enjoy an adult beverage at your hotel *before* you go out to dinner.

- Enjoy a lunch rather than a dinner at that five-star restaurant you've been dying to try. Lunch menus are usually about 30 to 50 percent less expensive than dinner fare.

- If you travel much at all on business or pleasure, membership almost always pays for itself (and more!) with the travel discounts you'll receive by joining organizations like AAA, AARP, and Hostelling International (see Cheap Shot). Even membership warehouse stores like Sam's Club and Costco offer discounts on travel services. If nothing else, flash your business card at hotels and see if they'll give you the corporate rate.

- Timing can be everything when it comes to finding travel bargains. Try staying at ski resorts in the summer and business hotels on the weekends. Or pack your bag first, then be surprised by where you'll be going with last-minute, deeply discounted travel deals on sites like LastMinuteTravel.com and Hotwire.com.

- See Chapter 9 for negotiating tips that might get you a break on hotels, rental cars, and even souvenirs during your trip. When you walk in without a reservation, hotels are often willing to cut you a better deal rather than risk leaving a room vacant for the night, but you need to ask. Also, remember that in many parts of the world it's considered impolite if you *don't* haggle when making a purchase—plus it's fun!

CHEAP SHOT
YOUTH HOSTELS FOR THE
YOUNG AT HEART

Cheapskate Bob Beard has truly seen the world, some parts of it many times over. It's fair to say he's visited pretty much all of the United States and Europe, not to mention China, Japan, Australia, New Zealand, South Africa, and the list goes on. How has Bob been able to travel the world on a teacher's salary? His secret is staying at youth hostels. You know, inexpensive places where young travelers can stay. The thing is, Bob just turned seventy-six, and he's still hostelling. "Now they're just called 'hostels,' since travelers of any age are welcome," Bob said, explaining that seniors and families are among the fastest-growing clientele at more than 4,000 hostels in the United States and around the world that are affiliated with the nonprofit organization Hostelling International (hiusa.org). Buy an annual membership for $28 ($18 for seniors, and free for kids under eighteen) and you'll have access to special discounts on travel and at hostels in more than eighty countries, which charge a nightly fee of about 80 percent less than hotels in the same locations. Plus you'll have use of the hostel's kitchen if you want to save even more by cooking some of your own meals.

Savings: Bob estimates that staying at hostels easily saves him **$1,000** on a two-week trip, compared to staying in hotels and eating in restaurants.

• Check out thrift stores and yard sales when you travel. You might find interesting souvenirs of the area that you'd never find in tourist shops or expensive gift shops. And consider buying apparel items during your travels as interesting souvenirs that you can literally carry on your back.

Vagabond traveler or value vigilante vacationer, one thing's for sure: The cheapskate next door saves up enough money (or credit card/frequent traveler points) to pay for vacations in advance.

"Save the amount needed before you go so you don't need to pay for it using credit cards," cheapskate Danny Kofke advises. You'll enjoy a stress-free vacation knowing it's already paid for; plus, saving up for a vacation all year long helps to build anticipation and get you excited about researching and planning your trip.

CHAPTER 16

Back to the Future?

**He is richest who is content with the least,
for content is the wealth of nature.**
—Socrates, apparently channeling Clive Jenkins

I may not know much, J.R., but I do know one thing: There's a difference between making a good living and making a good life. It's possible to have either one but not the other."

My friend and backyard barbecue master Clive Jenkins is a 260-pound living, breathing paradox. One minute he'll be asking—in all his endearingly blissful ignorance—something like, "Is Europe a country or a city?" Then the next thing you know he'll turn around and say something so profound it'll make you choke on the slab of venison brisket he just sliced off his homemade grilling rig.

In this instance, Clive was trying to console our friend J.R. Like so many Americans, J.R. recently lost a high-paying job. It was a job that he was proud of to the point of being boastful; not that there's anything wrong with that, but the sudden change in his personal demeanor after he got the job quickly earned him the surname "Ewing" among those of us who have known him for years. The job also allowed him to buy things for himself and for his family that seemed, at times, unnecessary to the point of being stupid. (Does a twelve-year-old—or anybody, for that matter—really need an ATV?) Maybe it was just coincidence, but during J.R.'s economic heyday, his wife of fourteen years decided to leave him.

Now J.R. is back at work at his old job, the one he had before "The Big Job." No, I'm not going to tell you he's happier now and got back together with his wife. J.R., like a lot of Americans these days, is having a hard time adjusting to living on less, to having to be less dependent on money and stuff in his pursuit of happiness. He talks openly about how he wished he'd put some of his pay in the bank when times were good; but, as he said, "I just thought it would never end, that every year I'd just keep making more and more money."

Life is different now for many Americans in this new economy, but only time will tell if it's better or worse. As we go forward and find out, it'll be worth keeping Clive's words in mind, not to mention those of that Socrates fellow.

Cheap: The Next Cool?

Those are the very same words that I used in the final chapter of my last book. At that time, suggesting that being cheap might come into fashion was as far-fetched as predicting that Lehman Brothers, Chrysler, and General Motors would all file for bankruptcy within a few months of each other.

But in fact, since the recession started, media outlets from the *New York Times* and the *Wall Street Journal* to *Newsweek*, *Time*, and every major television news network have carried headline stories proclaiming the same thing: Thrift/frugality/"being cheap" is now officially in vogue . . . again.

Did you know that for fifty years, up until 1966, America celebrated "National Thrift Week" (see bringbackthriftweek.org)? Yes, a national celebration that by its very essence didn't involve the buying and giving of gifts. In fact, it was a celebration of all things noncommercial—or, perhaps more accurately, a salute to responsible consumerism, smart saving, and sustainable living. The slogan for Thrift Week was "For Success and Happiness," recognizing that the word "thrift" has its roots in the phrase "to thrive."

It kicked off every year on January 17, the birthday of "America's apostle of thrift," Benjamin Franklin. Thrift Week celebrations were held in cities and towns across the country, with a different theme for every day of the week. You know, sexy topics, including: Have a Bank Account Day, Invest Safely Day, Carry Life Insurance Day, Keep a Budget Day, Pay Bills Promptly Day, Own Your Home Day, and Share with Others Day.

I don't know when or why thrift and frugality stopped being virtues in America and started being viewed as character flaws. I don't know when living within your means—let alone *below* your means—started seeming somehow un-American. When did we start believing that the best thing we can do for our country, let alone ourselves, is to go out and buy some stuff we don't need and can't afford, just so we can go out and do the same thing again tomorrow?

Certainly there must be more to life than that. The cheapskates next door think so, and maybe that's their biggest secret of all.

Upsides of the Down Economy

But now thrift is back, and hopefully it's here to stay. I am certainly not saying that economic downturn is a good thing. But if you believe as the cheapskates next door believe—namely, that most Americans would actually be happier, and the quality of their lives would increase, if they would only spend and consume less—then hard times will undoubtedly have a silver lining. Some upsides to the current down economy are already apparent:

- **We're borrowing less and putting more into savings.** We've learned a lesson—albeit the hard way—about living beyond our means. In 2008, personal savings rates rose to highs of over 6 percent, following the lowest savings rates since the Great Depression.

- **We're wasting less.** Sales at thrift stores like Goodwill stores are up by double digits compared to prior years. For the first time in decades, demand for used merchandise is exceeding the supply of donated items at many thrift stores.

- **We're building smaller homes.** It's good for your bank account—and good for the environment—not to construct, heat/cool, decorate, maintain, or pay taxes on extra square footage. In 2008, for the first time in more than ten years, the average size of new homes being built in the United States actually dropped by nearly three hundred square feet, or 11 percent.

- **We're driving less, staying around home more.** When gas was at $4 a gallon, two-thirds of Americans said they changed their habits and drove less . . . and nothing awful happened. Staying closer to home saves resources, generates less pollution, and stands to bring our families and communities closer together.

- **We're eating lower on the food chain, which is usually healthier.** Sales of poultry are up, of red meat down. We're buying more staples and fewer processed foods. We're eating more fruits and vegetables, and raising a lot more of those ourselves: The number of home vegetable gardens was up 40 percent in 2008 compared to 2007. If these trends continue, the next dire headline out of the recession might just be "American Obesity Epidemic Declines!"

Most of all, as we live our lives in both good times and bad, we need to remember that we live in a world where a third of the people are literally starving to death and almost half live on less than $2.50 a day. We need to always be thankful for what we do have, and think less, if at all, about what we don't.

There truly is a difference between making a good living and making a good life.

Thanks for Spending Some Time with the Cheapskates Next Door

Thanks for taking the time to read my book and get to know a little bit about the cheapskates next door.

I hope that if you're someone who doesn't yet live within or, better yet, *below* your means, this book has helped inspire you to give it a try. I hope it has given you some practical ideas for lifestyle changes you can make *right now* in order to simplify your life and make money a less important, less stressful part of it. I hope it has persuaded you that living more frugally isn't about sacrifice, it's about making choices every day that can actually increase the quality of your life and make you happier. As I've written elsewhere, "If you're looking for something more in life, you're likely to find it in something less."

If you're already a brother or sister of the Cheaphood—if you *are* the cheapskate next door—I appreciate you taking the time to read this book as well, and I look forward to receiving your comments and any ideas you'd like to share for how you enjoy life more by spending less. A final word of warning to the cheapskates next door: Don't be surprised to find a six-foot-four, bicycling cheap-skate on your doorstep some evening, wondering whether your couch is available for the night.

"Honey, lock the doors and draw the shades! The Ultimate Cheapskate's in town!"

SOURCES

Introduction

U.S. household debt at a record 133.7 percent of disposable income: Center for American Progress (americanprogress.org).

U.S. households with at least one credit card have nearly $10,700 in credit card debt: CardWeb.com.

U.S. college student debt of nearly $23,000: The College Board (CollegeBoard.com).

Growth in total U.S. consumer debt: U.S. Federal Reserve (federalreserve.gov).

U.S. household disposable income vs. savings: U.S. Bureau of Economic Analysis (bea.gov).

Spending to replace worn-out items: Betsy Morris, "Big Spenders: As a Favored Pastime, Shopping Ranks High with Most Americans," *Wall Street Journal,* July 30, 1987.

U.S. household net worth nosedive (2008): U.S. Federal Reserve (federalreserve.gov).

U.S. home values decline: Federal Housing Finance Agency (fhfa.gov).

U.S. bankruptcy filing (2008): Administrative Office of U.S. Courts (uscourts.gov).

U.S. unemployment rate (2009): U.S. Bureau of Labor Statistics (bls.gov).

Chapter 1: The Phrenology of Frugality

The impact of shopping less: Judith Levine, *Not Buying It: My Year without Shopping,* Free Press, 2007.

5,000 commercial messages per day: Louise Story, "Anywhere the Eye Can See, It's Likely to See an Ad," *New York Times,* January 15, 2007.

U.S. cell phone ownership: U.S. Census Bureau (census.gov).

Mortgage indebtedness: BankRate.com.

U.S. personal bankruptcies in more than one in a hundred households (2008): Administrative Office of U.S. Courts (uscourts.gov).

Chapter 2: Good Habits Are Hard to Break

U.S. national divorce rate: U.S. Census Bureau (census.gov).

U.S. purchases from vending machines: John Greenwood, "Point of Sale: The Vending Machine," *Financial Post,* December 2, 2008.

U.S. family of four's weekly spending: U.S. Census Bureau (census.gov).

Chapter 3: Money Management, Cheapskate Style

Charitable giving—U.S. average: The Center for Philanthropy at Indiana University (philanthropy.iupui.edu).

Chapter 4: The Oxygen Mask Approach to Raising Kids

$200,000+ to raise a child in the U.S.: BankRate.com.

U.S. household incomes—1970s vs. 2000s: U.S. Census Bureau (census .gov).

Average American home costs and size—1970s vs. 2000s: National Association of Home Builders (nahb.org).

Children directly and indirectly influence more than $700 billion in household spending: James McNeal, cited in "Marketing to Children," *The Economist,* November 30, 2006.

Hours spent watching television—average American family: The Nielsen Company (en-us.nielsen.com).

Student-loan debt statistics: The College Board (CollegeBoard.com).

Americans with at least a four-year college degree: U.S. Census Bureau (census.gov).

Average cost of college room and board: U.S. Department of Education (ed.gov).

U.S. spending on toys (annual): The NPD Group (npd.com).

Chapter 5: Thrift
Power leeches add 5 to 10 percent to average electrical bill: U.S. Department of Energy (energy.gov).

Oil used in manufacturing plastic water bottles: Earth Policy Institute (earth-policy.org).

Chapter 6: Clean Your Plate . . . and Save $1,500 a Year
World hunger statistics: Food and Agriculture Organization of the United Nations (fao.org).

U.S. household food-waste and spending: U.S. Department of Agriculture (usda.gov).

Chapter 8: We Can't Retire. We Went Out to Dinner Instead.
U.S. household spending on meals/beverages prepared outside the home: U.S. Bureau of Labor Statistics (bls.gov).

Chapter 9: The Joys of Horse Trading

Average cost of U.S. funeral: National Funeral Directors Association (nfda.org).

Chapter 10: Break the Mortgage Chains that Bind Thee

Average size of U.S. homes (historic trends): National Association of Home Builders (nahb.org).

Chapter 11: *Bon Appe-cheap!*

U.S. household spending on groceries: U.S. Department of Agriculture (usda.gov).

American grocery shopping habits and store practices: "Where the Rubber Meets the Road: A Model of In-Store Consumer Decision Making," a 1998 study by Russell S. Winer (University of California, Berkeley) and J. Jeffrey Inman (University of Wisconsin, Madison).

U.S. rate of vegetarianism: Vegetarian Resource Group (vrg.org).

Chapter 13: Cheapskates Come out of the Closet

U.S. household spending on clothing: U.S. Bureau of Labor Statistics (bls.gov).

Size of U.S. fashion industry: Council of Fashion Designers of America (CFDA.com).

Clothes thrown away in the U.S.: Earth911.com.

Size of U.S. dry cleaning industry: U.S. Dry Cleaning Corporation (usdrycleaning.com).

Chapter 14: Insurance

Americans without health insurance: U.S. Census Bureau (census.gov).

Decrease in term life insurance rates since mid-1990s: Insurance Information Institute (iii.org).

Chapter 15: Cheapskates Just Wanna Have Fun

U.S. citizens with passports: U.S. State Department (state.gov).

U.S. vs. European vacation trends: World at Work (WorldatWork .org).

Chapter 16: Back to the Future?

2008 personal savings rates increase: U.S. Commerce Department (commerce.gov).

Thrift store sales increase: Goodwill Industries International (goodwill .org).

Size of homes built in 2008 decreases: U.S. Census Bureau (census .gov).

Americans change driving habits with gas price increase: Survey by Ipsos Public Affairs on behalf of Access America Travel Insurance and Assistance (ipsos-na.com).

Increase in popularity of home vegetable gardens: National Gardening Association (garden.org).

World poverty statistics: World Bank (worldbank.org).

ABOUT THE AUTHOR

Jeff Yeager's first career was running nonprofit agencies, and he is now a writer and the creator of the website UltimateCheapskate.com. He has appeared on the *Today* show several times. His previous book, *The Ultimate Cheapskate's Road Map to True Riches*, was published by Broadway in 2007. He lives happily and frugally in Accokeek, Maryland, with his wife, Denise.